Cooking Light.
the Lazy
Gourmet

Cooking Light®
the Lazy Gourmet

Oxmoor
House®

Cooking Light®
the Lazy
Gourmet

ISBN: 0-8487-2708-8
Printed in the United States of America

Previously published as *The Lazy Gourmet*
© 1997 by Oxmoor House, Inc.

Be sure to check with your health-care provider
before making any changes in your diet.

Editor-in-Chief: Nancy Fitzpatrick Wyatt
Senior Foods Editor: Katherine M. Eakin
Senior Editor, Editorial Services: Olivia Kindig Wells
Art Director: James Boone

To order additional publications,
call 1-800-633-4910.

For more books to enrich your life, visit
oxmoorhouse.com

The Lazy Gourmet

Editors: Anne Chappell Cain, M.S., M.P.H., R.D.;
    Caroline A. Grant, M.S., R.D.
Copy Editor: Jacqueline Giovanelli
Editorial Assistant: Julie A. Cole
Designer: Carol Loria
Indexer: Keri Bradford Anderson
Proofreaders: Kathryn Stroud, Catherine S. Ritter

Director, Test Kitchens: Kathleen Royal Phillips
Assistant Director, Test Kitchens: Gayle Hays Sadler
Test Kitchen Home Economists: Molly Baldwin,
    Susan Hall Bellows, Julie Christopher,
    Michelle Brown Fuller, Natalie E. King,
    Elizabeth Tyler Luckett, Jan Jacks Moon,
    Iris Crawley O'Brien, Jan A. Smith
Recipe Developers: Oxmoor House Test Kitchen
    Home Economists; Alison Rich Lewis

Senior Photographer: Jim Bathie
Photographer: Ralph Anderson
Senior Photo Stylist: Kay E. Clarke
Photo Stylist: Virginia R. Cravens

Publishing Systems Administrator: Rick Tucker
Production and Distribution Director: Phillip Lee
Associate Production Manager: Theresa L. Beste
Production Assistant: Faye Porter Bonner

Cover: *Black Bean Lasagna Rolls (page 117)*
Page 1: *Italian Chicken Rolls (page 152)*
Page 2: *Stuffed Poblanos (page 120)*
Back cover: *Taco Burgers (page 124),
Frozen Lemon-Raspberry Pie (page 63),
Summertime Cookout (page 17)*

page 52

page 142

page 226

page 65

Contents

Welcome to the Lazy Gourmet kitchen!

It may come as a shock to my family and my friends, but it's not a goal in my life to spend every minute of my day in the kitchen creating fabulous healthy meals for their pleasure. After all, I do have a life! But I manage to put a fairly decent spread on the table every night without spending the whole day cooking. How? It's easy when you

- use no more than 7 ingredients (not including salt, pepper, water, or vegetable cooking spray)

- make the most of healthy convenience products

- create an entire meal from products that you already have in your kitchen

Good for You

Every recipe comes with a nutrient analysis so you can see how to fit the recipes into your healthy eating plan. (See *About the Recipes* on page 233 for more nutrient information.)

A Matter of Time

Each recipe has the prep time and the cook time listed under the recipe title to help you work the Lazy Gourmet recipes into your time schedule. **Prep Time** is the time you'll spend getting everything ready for the final dish, and the **Cook Time** is the time it takes to simmer, bake, broil, or grill the food. If you need to marinate, chill, or freeze, that time is listed, too.

Use my time-saving tips for whipping up unbelievable meals that are sure to bring rave reviews for your culinary skills.

It's as easy as 1 - 2 - 3 . . .

1 Stock Up

In addition to staples, condiments, and seasonings, I keep my kitchen stocked with healthy convenience products and basic quick-fix items. Here's the list I use for no-stress grocery shopping.

Eggs and Dairy
Eggs/Egg substitute
Cheese *(low-fat)*
Grated Parmesan cheese
Light process cream cheese
Milk, skim or 1% low-fat
Sour cream *(nonfat, low-fat)*
Yogurt *(fat-free, low-fat)*

Bread
Flour tortillas
French bread
Pita bread rounds
White or whole wheat
    bread

Baking Products
Biscuit and baking mix
    (reduced-fat)
Breadcrumbs, fine, dry
Corn muffin mix
Hot roll mix
Rapid-rise yeast

Grains
Couscous
Rice, quick-cooking,
    long-grain, and brown
Pasta, variety of shapes

Canned and Bottled Items
Beans *(no-salt-added)*
Broth, chicken and beef
    (no-salt-added)
Caramel-flavored syrup
    (fat-free)
Fruit, packed in juice
Fudge topping *(fat-free)*
Garlic, minced
Green chiles
Lemon juice
Maple syrup
    (reduced-calorie)
Pimiento, diced
Salsa *(no-salt-added)*
Soups *(reduced-sodium,*
    low-fat)
Spaghetti sauce *(fat-free)*
Tomato sauce and paste
    (no-salt-added)
Tomatoes, canned
    (no-salt-added)
Tuna, packed in water
    (low-sodium)

Condiments
Fruit spreads *(no-sugar-added)*
Mayonnaise *(nonfat, low-fat)*
Mustards, plain, flavored
Salad dressings *(fat-free,*
    low-fat)
Soy sauce/teriyaki sauce
    (low-sodium)
Vinegars
Worcestershire sauce
    (low-sodium)

Refrigerator
Breadstick dough
French bread dough
Pizza crust dough

Freezer
Assorted vegetables
Bread dough
Green pepper, chopped
Juice concentrates
Onion, chopped
Potatoes, mashed, hash
    brown
Vegetable blends
Whipped topping
    (low-calorie)

Grocery Shopping Stress Busters

■ Try to plan and shop for a week's worth of meals. It might take a few extra minutes initially, but once you're in the habit of planning weekly menus, you'll save time and reduce the stress of coming up with meal ideas at the last minute.

■ Keep a notepad and pencil in the kitchen (a magnet-backed pad on the refrigerator is handy) to jot down the items that are running low.

2 Pare Down

Get rid of all the kitchenware you never use, and pare down to the basics. I've found that a few key items help me save time and energy in the kitchen.

Aluminum foil
Blender
Bread machine
Electric slow cooker
Food processor
Garlic peeler
Gas grill
Graduated measuring cups
Graduated measuring spoons
Kitchen shears

Knife set
Microwave oven
Mini food chopper
Mushroom slicer
Nonstick skillets
Pizza cutter
Pressure cooker
Steamer basket
Vegetable peeler
Wok
Zip-top plastic bags

Mini food chopper

3 Take Shortcuts

I don't believe in spending more time or effort in the kitchen than I absolutely have to, so here are a few of my shortcuts. They may seem simple, but they work!

◄ Use a mushroom slicer to quickly slice whole mushrooms, strawberries, and hard-cooked eggs.

◄ Line the bottom of a broiler pan with aluminum foil for easy clean up.

Use heavy-duty, zip-top plastic bags for recipe shortcuts.

◄ Remove fat from pan liquids. Pour the pan drippings and liquid into the bag. Let the fat rise to the top. Snip off one bottom corner of the bag, and pour out the fat-free broth. The fat will stay in the plastic bag.

■ Use a zip-top plastic bag to make crumbs for toppings. Place cereal or cookies in the bag; crush the contents of the bag into crumbs with your hands or a rolling pin.

◄ Marinate meat or poultry. Turn the bag occasionally to completely coat the food.

◄ Drizzle melted chocolate over desserts. Use the microwave to melt the chocolate in the bag; snip off one bottom corner to form a small hole, and squeeze.

continued

◀ Spray measuring cups and spoons with vegetable cooking spray before measuring sticky ingredients such as honey or peanut butter. It helps the ingredient to come out of the measuring cup easily.

◀ Use a pizza cutter to cut refrigerated bread doughs and tortillas.

■ If you have a self-cleaning oven, put dirty grill racks in the oven before you clean it.

◀ Use a graduated measuring spoon or cup. It's one spoon or one cup that adjusts for the measurement you need so you don't have to mess up a whole set.

■ To quickly shred fresh spinach or basil, stack several leaves on top of each other; roll them into a cylinder-like shape, and slice cross-wise into shreds.

◀ To get thin strips from a green pepper in a hurry, slice the pepper from stem to bottom on 4 sides of the pepper to get 4 rectangular pieces of pepper. Place one piece on top of the other and slice into strips.

◀ Try this simple gadget for peeling garlic cloves. Just put a clove in the pliable plastic tube, and roll it back and forth. Remove the garlic, and the skin falls away. No mess and no garlic-scented fingers.

■ Buy foods in user-friendly forms such as prewashed and trimmed spinach, sliced fresh mushrooms, and peeled and deveined shrimp. Check the supermarket salad bar for chopped and sliced fruits and vegetables.

■ Spray a rubber spatula with cooking spray before stirring tomato-based products. This will keep the sauce from staining the spatula.

Use kitchen shears to speed up food preparation.

◀ Chop canned tomatoes right in the can.

■ Cut Cornish hens in half if you don't have an electric knife.

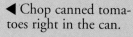

◀ Chop dried fruit and sun-dried tomatoes with shears coated with vegetable cooking spray.

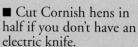

■ Trim fat from meat.

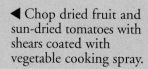

■ Chop or mince herbs in a glass measuring cup.

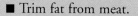

◀ Use a vegetable peeler to shave Parmesan cheese and chocolate.

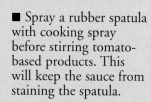

Gourmet Meals in Minutes

A menu is simply three or four items that go together to make up a meal. There is no rule that says you must start from scratch and prepare a recipe for every item.

Give yourself a break: Make the entrée, and add bread from the bakery and salad from a bag. Grill a tenderloin and serve it with steamed veggies. And if you offer dessert, take a shortcut with commercial products.

The following seven menus feature some of my favorite recipes from this cookbook, and they meet my Lazy Gourmet standards for menus:

■ Low fat and low calorie: Each menu lists the total calories per serving and the percent of calories from fat. Every menu is below 30 percent calories from fat.

■ Easy enough to make when you get home from work: To make meal planning even easier, each menu has its own grocery list and a step-by-step plan that helps you pull the meal together perfectly every time.

■ Special enough for company: Each menu photograph includes a simple idea for serving the meal with style. I hope that my suggestions will inspire you to create your own style as you add "That Special Touch" to your meals.

Prepare meals in minutes? Yes, you can!

That Special Touch

Use an herb pot basket as an apple holder, and let crisp fall apples be the centerpiece and the dessert.

Soup and Sandwich Break

■ ■ ■

Spicy Tomato-Corn Chowder, page 225

Glorified Grilled Cheese, page 190

Apples (1 per serving)

Serves 4
Total calories per serving: 514
Percent calories from fat: 23%

■ ■ ■

What You'll Need

Staples: Reduced-calorie margarine, nonfat sour cream, canned no-salt-added chicken broth, hot sauce, dried basil, salt, pepper, vegetable cooking spray

Groceries:
4 apples
⅓ cup Neufchâtel cheese
4 slices fat-free sharp Cheddar cheese
4 slices fat-free mozzarella cheese
1 (10¾-ounce) can reduced-fat, reduced-sodium
    tomato soup
Roasted garlic-flavored vegetable oil
1 (10-ounce) package frozen whole-kernel corn
8 slices white or whole wheat bread

Making It Happen

1 Thaw the frozen corn; then sauté the corn and basil.

2 Combine the ingredients for the chowder.

3 While the chowder simmers, cook the cheese sandwiches.

Light Vegetarian Lunch

■ ■ ■

Grecian Stuffed Potatoes, page 112

Spinach-orange salad (1½ cups per serving)

Fat-free oatmeal-raisin cookies (2 per serving)

Serves 4
Total calories per serving: 519
Percent calories from fat: 12%

■ ■ ■

What You'll Need

Staples: Lemon juice, no-salt-added Greek seasoning, salt, pepper

Groceries:
4 baking potatoes
2 large tomatoes
1 package torn fresh spinach (about 6 cups)
1 purple onion
1 medium orange
½ cup reduced-fat feta cheese
1 (2¼-ounce) can sliced ripe olives
1 (15-ounce) can no-salt-added garbanzo beans
Fat-free olive oil vinaigrette
1 package fat-free oatmeal-raisin cookies

Making It Happen

1 Bake the potatoes in the oven or the microwave oven.

2 While the potatoes bake, combine the ingredients for the potato topping.

3 Toss the following ingredients for a quick spinach salad:
   6 cups torn fresh spinach
   1 purple onion, sliced into rings
   1 orange, peeled and cut into wedges
   ½ cup fat-free olive oil vinaigrette.

4 Top the potatoes, and serve.

That Special Touch

Pick some flowers from the yard, and tie ribbons around the stems to make little bouquets for each place setting.

Summertime Cookout

■ ■ ■

Grilled Firecracker Chicken, page 154

Cheddar Scalloped Potatoes, page 215

Melon-Cucumber Salad, page 170

Serves 4
Total calories per serving: 424
Percent calories from fat: 16%

■ ■ ■

What You'll Need

Staples: Reduced-calorie margarine, skim milk, lemon juice, no-salt-added tomato sauce, flour, vegetable oil, chili powder, ground red pepper, garlic powder, salt, vegetable cooking spray

Groceries:
4 (4-ounce) skinned, boned chicken breast halves
1 large cantaloupe
1 medium cucumber
1 pound baking potatoes
4 green onions
⅓ cup shredded reduced-fat sharp Cheddar cheese
1 (7-ounce) can jalapeño peppers
No-sugar-added apple jelly
1 (6-ounce) can frozen limeade concentrate

Making It Happen

1 Prepare the melon salad, and let it chill.

2 Marinate the chicken for 15 minutes. While the chicken marinates, fire up the grill.

3 Prepare the potatoes, and cook them in the microwave oven.

4 Keep the potatoes warm while you grill the chicken.

That Special Touch

Brighten the table with sweet red peppers, and put fortune cookies in straw boxes on the table. Let everybody read their fortune as they enjoy the cookies and hot tea for dessert.

Asian Dinner

■ ■ ■

Indonesian Pork Tenderloin, page 144

Hot Sesame Spaghetti, page 102

Fresh orange wedges (2 per serving)

Fortune cookies (1 per serving)

Hot tea

Serves 4
Total calories per serving: 466
Percent calories from fat: 20%

■ ■ ■

What You'll Need

Staples: Low-sodium soy sauce, hot chile oil, garlic cloves, vegetable cooking spray, dried crushed red pepper, salt, tea bags

Groceries:
1 (1-pound) pork tenderloin
2½ cups broccoli flowerets
1 large sweet red pepper
2 green onions
1 medium orange
8 ounces spaghetti
Reduced-fat creamy peanut butter
Pineapple preserves
Sesame seeds
Fortune cookies

Making It Happen

1 Chop the vegetables for the spaghetti.

2 Prepare and cook the pork tenderloin.

3 Cook the spaghetti while the pork is cooking.

4 Combine the spaghetti and chopped vegetables.

That Special Touch

Use small pots of fresh herbs on the table for a fresh-from-the-garden look. For a taller arrangement, plant herbs in a unique container like an antique watering can.

Supper on the Bayou

■ ■ ■

Cajun-Spiced Catfish, page 77

Steamed broccoli (1 cup per serving)

Parslied potatoes (3 per serving)

Cheddar Drop Biscuits, page 46 (1 per serving)

Strawberry sorbet (¹/₂ cup per serving)

Serves 4
Total calories per serving: 479
Percent calories from fat: 26%

■ ■ ■

What You'll Need

Staples: Reduced-calorie margarine, skim milk, ground red pepper, dried basil, dried parsley, dried thyme, garlic powder, paprika, salt, pepper, vegetable cooking spray

Groceries:
4 (4-ounce) catfish fillets
12 small round red potatoes
4 cups broccoli flowerets
Fresh parsley
¹/₂ cup shredded reduced-fat sharp Cheddar cheese
Strawberry sorbet
Reduced-fat biscuit and baking mix

Making It Happen

1 Quarter the potatoes, and cook them in boiling water to cover for 15 minutes.

2 Make the biscuits while the potatoes cook. Remove the biscuits from the oven, and keep them warm.

3 Top the fish with the seasoning mixture. Cook the broccoli in the microwave while the fish is broiling.

4 Toss the potatoes with 2 teaspoons of melted margarine and fresh parsley just before serving.

That Special Touch

Turn a condiment holder into a candle holder, and light the candles for a romantic dinner. To add a finishing touch, adorn the table with fresh limes and paperwhites.

Anniversary Celebration

■ ■ ■

Veal in Lime Cream Sauce, page 138

Roasted Garlic and Onion Linguine, page 100

Steamed Sugar Snap peas (¹/₂ cup per serving)

Whole wheat rolls (1 per serving)

Fat-free chocolate pound cake (1 slice per serving)

White wine (6 fluid ounces per serving)

Serves 4
Total calories per serving: 794
Percent calories from fat: 12%

■ ■ ■

What You'll Need

Staples: Evaporated skimmed milk, flour, low-sodium and no-salt-added chicken broths, cracked black pepper, salt, pepper, olive oil-flavored and butter-flavored vegetable cooking sprays, olive oil

Groceries:
1 pound veal cutlets
4 cups Sugar Snap peas
2 small onions
2 limes
¼ cup grated Parmesan cheese
1 small head garlic
12 ounces linguine
1 (15-ounce) loaf fat-free chocolate pound cake
4 whole wheat rolls
1 bottle dry white wine

Making It Happen

1 Roast the onion and garlic for the pasta dish.

2 After the onion and garlic have been roasting for about 30 minutes, brown the veal.

3 Process the garlic mixture.

4 Boil the water for the linguine, and let it cook while you prepare the cream sauce. Add the veal to the sauce.

5 Just before serving, steam the peas, and heat the rolls.

That Special Touch

Arrange shafts of wheat or tall grasses cut from the sides of the road in a vase instead of flowers for a centerpiece. Serve the beverages in pewter steins or goblets.

Oktoberfest Feast

■ ■ ■

Roasted Reuben Tenderloin, page 131

Caraway-Swiss Casserole Bread, page 49 (1 slice per serving)

Steamed green beans (1 cup per serving)

Watercress and fruit salad (1½ cups per serving)

Light beer (12 fluid ounces per serving)

Serves 12
Total calories per serving: 602
Percent calories from fat: 22%

■ ■ ■

What You'll Need

Staples: Margarine, cracked black pepper, caraway seeds, ground allspice, vegetable cooking spray

Groceries:
1 (3-pound) beef tenderloin
4 red apples
3 pears
3 pounds fresh or frozen green beans
12 cups torn fresh watercress
1 large onion
1 cup shredded reduced-fat Swiss cheese
3 ounces fresh Parmesan cheese
Fat-free balsamic vinaigrette
Fat-free Thousand Island dressing
1½ cups sauerkraut
1 (16-ounce) package hot roll mix
2 slices rye bread
Light beer

Making It Happen

1 Prepare the bread first. While it rises and bakes, assemble the stuffed tenderloin.

2 Roast the tenderloin for 50 minutes.

3 Toss the following ingredients for the salad:
   12 cups torn fresh watercress
   3 red apples, sliced
   3 pears, sliced
   3 ounces fresh Parmesan cheese, shredded
   ¾ cup fat-free balsamic vinaigrette.

4 Steam the green beans while the tenderloin stands.

Appetizers

▪ ▪ ▪

Beverages

OK. So I didn't snip the herbs from the garden or bake the bread in a hearth oven (it came out of a plastic wrapper). And I certainly didn't have the time to peel the shrimp, so I asked the grocer to do it. But the last time I served Shrimp Canapés, every morsel was eaten, and my guests were clamoring for more.

With the grocer's help on the shrimp, it took only 15 minutes and 7 ingredients to create these tasty morsels. I'm no fool.

Shrimp Canapés (page 32) and
Minted Orange-Lemon Fizz (page 37)

27

■ Any canned fruit from your pantry, such as apricots, peaches, or pears, will do in this dip. You'll need about ½ cup chopped, drained fruit.

Orange Dip

Prep: 10 minutes

1 (8-ounce) carton vanilla low-fat yogurt
3 tablespoons light process cream cheese, softened
1 (11-ounce) can mandarin oranges in light syrup, drained
    and chopped
1 teaspoon sugar
2 teaspoons fresh lime juice

1 Spoon yogurt onto several layers of heavy-duty paper towels; spread to ½-inch thickness. Cover with additional paper towels; let stand 5 minutes.

2 Scrape yogurt into a bowl, using a rubber spatula. Add cream cheese and remaining ingredients, stirring well with a wire whisk until blended. Serve with fresh fruit such as apple or pear slices, strawberries, or pineapple chunks.
Yield: 1 cup.

Per Tablespoon: Calories 23 (23% from fat)   Fat 0.6g (Sat 0.3g)   Protein 0.9g   Carbohydrate 3.8g   Fiber 0.0g   Cholesterol 2mg   Sodium 22mg

Yogurt Fit for a Dip

Use this quick method for draining yogurt so that it will be the right consistency for a dip. (You'll be surprised by the amount of liquid that is absorbed by the towels.) Eight ounces of yogurt will equal about ½ cup of drained yogurt. It will be the consistency of very soft cream cheese.

Spoon the yogurt onto a stack of at least three paper towels, and spread with a spatula.

Cover the yogurt with two or more paper towels, and let it stand 5 minutes.

Scrape the thickened yogurt into a bowl using a spatula.

Red Bean Hummus with Pita Wedges

Prep: 12 minutes

3 cloves garlic
1 (16-ounce) can red beans, drained
2 tablespoons fresh lime juice
2 teaspoons sesame oil
¼ teaspoon ground cumin
3 (6-inch) pita bread rounds

1 Position knife blade in food processor bowl. Drop garlic through food chute with processor running; process 3 seconds or until garlic is minced. Add beans and next 3 ingredients; process until smooth.

2 Separate each pita bread round into 2 rounds; cut each into 8 wedges. Serve hummus with pita wedges.
Yield: 24 appetizer servings (serving size: 1 tablespoon dip and 2 pita wedges).

Per Serving: Calories 47 (11% from fat)   Fat 0.6g (Sat 0.1g)   Protein 1.7g
Carbohydrate 8.2g   Fiber 1.4g   Cholesterol 0mg   Sodium 49mg

■ Red beans give hummus (a Middle Eastern dip made with garbanzo beans) a new twist. Like traditional hummus, this dip has a powerful garlic punch.

Sweet Onion Spread

Prep: 5 minutes

⅔ cup light process cream cheese, softened
¼ cup plus 2 tablespoons sweet onion relish
2 tablespoons nonfat mayonnaise
¼ teaspoon pepper

1 Combine all ingredients, stirring well. Serve spread with assorted low-fat crackers.
Yield: 1 cup.

Per Tablespoon: Calories 16 (45% from fat)   Fat 0.8g (Sat 0.5g)   Protein 0.5g
Carbohydrate 2.0g   Fiber 0.0g   Cholesterol 3mg   Sodium 50mg

■ Spread this creamy onion mixture on ham and Swiss hoagies or roast beef sandwiches in place of mayonnaise or mustard.

If you use frozen chopped pepper, thaw it and drain well to get rid of excess moisture.

Pineapple Cheese Ball

Prep: 15 minutes   Chill: 30 minutes; 3 hours

¾ cup (3 ounces) shredded fat-free sharp Cheddar cheese
½ cup finely chopped green pepper
2 teaspoons grated onion
1 (8-ounce) can crushed pineapple in juice, well drained
½ (8-ounce) package Neufchâtel cheese, softened
½ (8-ounce) package fat-free cream cheese, softened
⅔ cup chopped fresh parsley

1 Combine first 6 ingredients in a medium bowl. Cover and chill 30 minutes.

2 Shape cheese mixture into a ball; roll in chopped parsley, coating thoroughly. Cover and chill thoroughly. Serve with Melba toast rounds or fat-free crackers.
Yield: 2¼ cups.

Per Tablespoon: Calories 17 (42% from fat)   Fat 0.8g (Sat 0.5g)   Protein 1.6g   Carbohydrate 0.9g   Fiber 0.1g   Cholesterol 3mg   Sodium 49mg

One baguette (a long skinny loaf of French bread) will give you 24 little toasts that are just the right size for pick-up food.

Garlic-Cheese Toasts

Prep: 10 minutes

½ cup light process cream cheese, softened
1 tablespoon plus 1½ teaspoons chopped fresh chives
1 tablespoon grated fat-free Parmesan topping
1 clove garlic, minced
24 (½-inch-thick) slices French baguette, toasted

1 Combine first 4 ingredients in a small bowl, stirring until smooth. Spread 1 teaspoon cream cheese mixture over one side of each toasted baguette slice.
Yield: 24 appetizers.

Per Appetizer: Calories 36 (25% from fat)   Fat 1.0g (Sat 0.5g)   Protein 1.4g   Carbohydrate 5.2g   Fiber 0.1g   Cholesterol 3mg   Sodium 79mg

Shrimp-Chutney Spread

Prep: 20 minutes   Chill: 30 minutes

3 cups water
1 pound unpeeled medium-size fresh shrimp
1 (8-ounce) container light process cream cheese, softened
½ cup nonfat sour cream
¼ cup finely chopped green onions
¼ cup mango chutney
1 tablespoon curry powder
¼ teaspoon salt
⅛ teaspoon ground white pepper
1 clove garlic, minced
Green onion curls (optional)

1 Bring water to a boil in a large saucepan; add shrimp, and cook 3 to 5 minutes or until shrimp turn pink. Drain well; rinse with cold water. Chill. Peel, devein, and finely chop shrimp. (If desired, peel one shrimp, leaving tail intact; set aside for garnish.)

2 Combine cream cheese and next 7 ingredients in a medium bowl; beat at medium speed of an electric mixer until blended. Stir in chopped shrimp. Serve with low-fat crackers and raw fresh vegetables. If desired, garnish with reserved shrimp and green onion curls.
Yield: 2¾ cups.

Per Tablespoon: Calories 26 (35% from fat)   Fat 1.0g (Sat 0.5g)   Protein 2.3g
Carbohydrate 1.9g   Fiber 0.1g   Cholesterol 17mg   Sodium 76mg

■ Buy cooked shrimp from the grocery store and decrease your prep time by 15 minutes. It may cost a little more, but your time may be worth the extra pennies.

*Shrimp-Chutney
Spread*

Look for the phyllo shells in the freezer section of your grocery store.

Crabmeat and Bacon Cups

Prep: 25 minutes   Chill: 1 hour

2 slices turkey bacon, cooked and crumbled
½ pound fresh crabmeat, drained and flaked
¼ cup nonfat sour cream
¼ cup nonfat mayonnaise
1½ teaspoons fresh or frozen chopped chives
¼ teaspoon pepper
2 (2.1-ounce) packages frozen miniature phyllo shells, thawed

1 Combine first 6 ingredients, stirring well. Cover and chill. To serve, spoon crabmeat mixture into phyllo shells.
Yield: 30 appetizers.

Per Appetizer: Calories 35 (32% from fat)   Fat 1.3g (Sat 0.1g)   Protein 2.3g
Carbohydrate 3.2g   Fiber 0.0g   Cholesterol 8mg   Sodium 69mg

Canapé is the French word for couch. If you need more time to relax on yours, cut the prep time for these decorative little party sandwiches by having the grocer peel and devein the shrimp.

Shrimp Canapés

Prep: 25 minutes   Chill: 2 hours

12 unpeeled medium-size fresh shrimp
½ cup plus 1 teaspoon dry white wine, divided
½ cup canned no-salt-added chicken broth
2 fresh dillweed sprigs
6 (1-ounce) slices whole wheat bread
¼ cup light process cream cheese
1½ teaspoons minced fresh dillweed
Fresh dillweed sprigs (optional)

1 Peel and devein shrimp, leaving tails on, if desired. Combine ½ cup wine, broth, and 2 dillweed sprigs in a medium saucepan. Bring to a boil; add shrimp, and cook 3 to 4 minutes or until shrimp turn pink. Transfer shrimp and liquid to a bowl. Cover and chill thoroughly.

2 Cut bread slices into 12 rounds with a 2-inch biscuit cutter. Reserve remaining bread pieces for another use. Place bread rounds on a baking sheet. Broil 5½ inches from heat (with electric oven door partially opened) 1 minute on each side or until lightly toasted.

3 Combine cream cheese, minced dillweed, and remaining 1 teaspoon wine. Spread cheese mixture evenly over one side of bread rounds. Remove shrimp from liquid; discard liquid. Place one shrimp on each bread round. Garnish with fresh dillweed sprigs, if desired.
Yield: 12 appetizers.   *(Recipe pictured on page 26.)*

Per Appetizer: Calories 30 (30% from fat)   Fat 1.0g (Sat 0.5g)   Protein 2.6g
Carbohydrate 2.7g   Fiber 0.2g   Cholesterol 18mg   Sodium 69mg

Peppered Tuna Bruschetta

Prep: 18 minutes   Cook: 10 minutes

1½ tablespoons olive oil, divided
4 (4-ounce) fresh tuna steaks
1 teaspoon freshly ground pepper
Olive oil-flavored vegetable cooking spray
1 (12-ounce) jar roasted red peppers in water
1 tablespoon chopped fresh tarragon
1 tablespoon fresh lemon juice
2 large cloves garlic, divided
30 (½-inch-thick) slices French baguette

1 Brush 1½ teaspoons olive oil evenly over tuna steaks. Sprinkle
1 teaspoon pepper over both sides of tuna, pressing pepper into tuna.

2 Coat grill rack with cooking spray; place on grill over medium-
hot coals (350° to 400°). Place tuna on rack; grill, covered, 4 minutes
on each side or until fish flakes easily when tested with a fork.

3 Flake tuna in a medium bowl. Drain red peppers, reserving liquid.
Chop enough peppers to measure ¾ cup. Reserve remaining peppers
and liquid for another use. Add chopped peppers, remaining 1 tablespoon olive oil, tarragon, and lemon juice to tuna, stirring lightly.
Finely chop 1 clove garlic; add to tuna mixture. Set aside.

4 Lightly coat both sides of bread slices with cooking spray. Cut
remaining 1 clove garlic in half; rub bread slices with cut sides of
garlic. Arrange bread slices in a single layer on a baking sheet. Bake
at 350° for 10 minutes or until lightly browned, turning once. Spoon
tuna mixture evenly over bread slices.
Yield: 30 appetizers.

Per Appetizer: Calories 61 (25% from fat)   Fat 1.7g (Sat 0.4g)   Protein 4.4g
Carbohydrate 6.4g   Fiber 0.3g   Cholesterol 6mg   Sodium 78mg

■ The flavor of the grilled
fresh tuna is the best part of
this bruschetta (Italian for
roasted garlic bread) topping.
But if you're in a real time
crunch, use 2 (6-ounce) cans
of low-salt white tuna instead.

White Chili Snackers

White Chili Snackers

Prep: 36 minutes   Cook: 5 minutes

2 (4-ounce) packages roast-flavored chicken breast halves
1 (15-ounce) can Great Northern beans, drained
¼ teaspoon ground cumin
20 (3-inch) crackerbread rounds (or water crackers)
½ cup tomatillo salsa
½ cup (2 ounces) shredded reduced-fat Monterey Jack cheese
Cherry tomato wedges (optional)
Fresh cilantro leaves (optional)

1 Broil chicken according to package directions; let cool slightly. Shred chicken, and set aside.

2 Position knife blade in food processor bowl; add beans and cumin. Process 1½ minutes. Spread mixture over crackers; top with salsa and chicken. Sprinkle with cheese. Place on a baking sheet; bake at 400° for 5 minutes. If desired, garnish with tomato and cilantro. **Yield: 20 appetizers.**

Per Appetizer: Calories 52 (17% from fat)   Fat 1.0g (Sat 0.4)   Protein 4.5g Carbohydrate 6.5g   Fiber 0.8g   Cholesterol 7mg   Sodium 147mg

■ Look for roast-flavored chicken breast halves (such as Chicken by George) in the fresh poultry section of the grocery store. If you can't find them, use roasted chicken from the deli. You'll need about 6 ounces of cooked chicken.

Santa Fe Chicken Quesadillas

Prep: 10 minutes   Cook: 12 minutes

1¼ cups no-salt-added salsa, divided
1 cup chopped cooked chicken breast (skinned before cooking
       and cooked without salt)
2 tablespoons chopped fresh cilantro
1 teaspoon ground cumin
1 (4-ounce) can chopped green chiles, drained
6 (7-inch) flour tortillas
1 cup (4 ounces) shredded reduced-fat sharp Cheddar cheese
Vegetable cooking spray

1 Combine ½ cup salsa, chicken, and next 3 ingredients. Spoon mixture evenly onto one half of each tortilla. Sprinkle with cheese.

2 Coat a nonstick skillet with cooking spray; place over medium-high heat until hot. Add one tortilla; cook 1 minute. Fold in half; cook 30 seconds. Turn; cook other side 30 seconds. Repeat with remaining tortillas. Cut each into 4 wedges. Top with ¾ cup salsa. **Yield: 2 dozen appetizers.**

Per Appetizer: Calories 61 (28% from fat)   Fat 1.9g (Sat 0.7g)   Protein 4.6g Carbohydrate 6.3g   Fiber 0.3g   Cholesterol 9mg   Sodium 129mg

When fresh peaches aren't in season, use a 16-ounce package of frozen sliced peaches.

Peachy Champagne Coolers

Prep: 10 minutes   Freeze: 1 hour

3½ cups peeled, sliced fresh peaches (about 5 medium)
1 (12-ounce) can peach nectar
2 cups chilled champagne

1 Place sliced fresh peaches in a single layer on a baking sheet. Cover and freeze for 1 hour.

2 Combine peach slices and nectar in container of an electric blender; cover and process until smooth. Pour into a large pitcher. Slowly add champagne to peach mixture, stirring lightly. Pour into chilled champagne glasses. Serve immediately.
Yield: 6 (1-cup) servings.

Per Serving: Calories 123 (1% from fat)   Fat 0.2g (Sat 0.0g)   Protein 0.9g   Carbohydrate 17.4g   Fiber 1.3g   Cholesterol 0mg   Sodium 7mg

If you can't find low-fat butter pecan ice cream, it's easy to make your own with low-fat vanilla ice cream, ⅛ teaspoon butter-flavored extract, and ¼ cup finely chopped pecans.

Buttered Rum Milk Shakes

Prep: 5 minutes

3 cups low-fat butter pecan ice cream
2 cups ice cubes
½ cup skim milk
1 tablespoon dark rum

1 Combine ice cream, ice cubes, milk, and rum in container of an electric blender; cover and process until smooth. Serve immediately.
Yield: 4 (1-cup) servings.

Per Serving: Calories 199 (14% from fat)   Fat 3.1g (Sat 1.5g)   Protein 5.6g   Carbohydrate 34.5g   Fiber 1.5g   Cholesterol 1mg   Sodium 106mg

Minted Orange-Lemon Fizz

Prep: 20 minutes   Chill: 1 to 3 hours

1¼ cups water
⅔ cup sugar
½ cup tightly packed mint leaves
1 tablespoon grated orange rind
¾ cup unsweetened orange juice
¾ cup fresh lemon juice
2 cups lemon-flavored sparkling water, chilled
Fresh mint sprigs (optional)

1 Combine 1¼ cups water and sugar in a small saucepan; cook over medium heat, stirring constantly, until sugar dissolves. Remove from heat, and let cool completely.

2 Combine sugar mixture, ½ cup mint leaves, and next 3 ingredients. Cover and chill.

3 Pour mixture through a wire-mesh strainer into a pitcher, discarding mint and orange rind. Just before serving, stir in sparkling water. Serve over ice. Garnish with fresh mint sprigs, if desired.
Yield: 5 (1-cup) servings.   *(Recipe pictured on page 26.)*

Per Serving: Calories 128 (0% from fat)   Fat 0.0g (Sat 0.0g)   Protein 0.4g
Carbohydrate 33.6g   Fiber 0.1g   Cholesterol 0mg   Sodium 21mg

■ You can make the orange syrup mixture a day ahead to get even more flavor from the mint leaves.

Hawaiian Crush

Prep: 5 minutes

1¾ cups guava nectar
¾ cup water
1 (12-ounce) can frozen pineapple juice concentrate, thawed and undiluted
¼ teaspoon coconut extract
1 (33.8-ounce) bottle club soda, chilled

1 Combine first 4 ingredients in a large pitcher, stirring well. Cover and chill, if desired.

2 Just before serving, stir in club soda. Serve over crushed ice.
Yield: 8 (1-cup) servings.

Per Serving: Calories 110 (0% from fat)   Fat 0.0g (Sat 0.0g)   Protein 0.5g
Carbohydrate 27.2g   Fiber 0.5g   Cholesterol 0mg   Sodium 28mg

■ You'll get a more authentic island flavor with the guava nectar, but peach nectar is a good substitute.

Cherry Limeade

Prep: 2 minutes   Chill: 1 to 2 hours

1 (6-ounce) jar maraschino cherries with stems
1 (6-ounce) can frozen limeade concentrate, thawed and undiluted
1 cup water
2 cups lime-flavored sparkling water, chilled
Lime slices (optional)

1 Drain cherries, reserving ⅓ cup juice. Set aside 8 cherries, reserving remaining cherries for another use.

2 Combine ⅓ cup cherry juice, limeade concentrate, and 1 cup water in a pitcher. Cover and chill thoroughly.

3 Just before serving, stir in sparkling water. Serve with cherries over crushed ice. Garnish with lime slices, if desired.
Yield: 4 (1-cup) servings.

Per Serving: Calories 149 (0% from fat)   Fat 0.0g (Sat 0.0g)   Protein 0.1g
Carbohydrate 35.0g   Fiber 0.0g   Cholesterol 0mg   Sodium 18mg

Cherry Limeade

Mulled Cider Supreme

Prep: 10 minutes   Cook: 15 minutes

4½ cups unsweetened apple cider
1 cup water
2 tablespoons brown sugar
2 (3-inch) sticks cinnamon
5 whole cloves
3 whole allspice
2 tablespoons crystallized ginger
1 (2-inch) piece peeled gingerroot

1 Combine first 3 ingredients in a saucepan, stirring well.

2 Place cinnamon sticks and remaining 4 ingredients on a 6-inch square of cheesecloth; tie with string.

3 Add spice bag to cider mixture. Bring to a simmer over medium-high heat, stirring occasionally. Reduce heat to low; cook, uncovered, 15 minutes, stirring occasionally. Remove and discard spice bag. Pour cider mixture into individual mugs. Serve warm.
Yield: 5 (1-cup) servings.

Per Serving: Calories 126 (1% from fat)   Fat 0.2g (Sat 0.0g)   Protein 0.1g
Carbohydrate 31.4g   Fiber 0.4g   Cholesterol 0mg   Sodium 9mg

Caramel-Nut Coffee Coolers

Prep: 5 minutes   Chill: 1 hour

2½ cups brewed coffee
3 tablespoons fat-free caramel-flavored syrup
½ cup refrigerated fat-free hazelnut-flavored nondairy coffee
    creamer
¼ cup frozen reduced-calorie whipped topping, thawed
2 teaspoons fat-free caramel-flavored syrup

1 Combine coffee and 3 tablespoons caramel syrup, stirring until syrup dissolves. Stir in creamer; cover and chill.

2 Pour coffee mixture evenly into four glasses. Top each serving with 1 tablespoon whipped topping; drizzle evenly with 2 teaspoons syrup. Serve immediately.
Yield: 4 (¾-cup) servings.

Per Serving: Calories 134 (4% from fat)   Fat 0.6g (Sat 0.5g)   Protein 0.3g
Carbohydrate 28.9g   Fiber 0.0g   Cholesterol 0mg   Sodium 56mg

Bundle Up

Spices tied up in cheesecloth or in a piece of a coffee filter are easier to remove from the saucepan after simmering.

Place the spices in the center of the cheesecloth square.

Tie the cheesecloth around the spices with a piece of string, making a bundle.

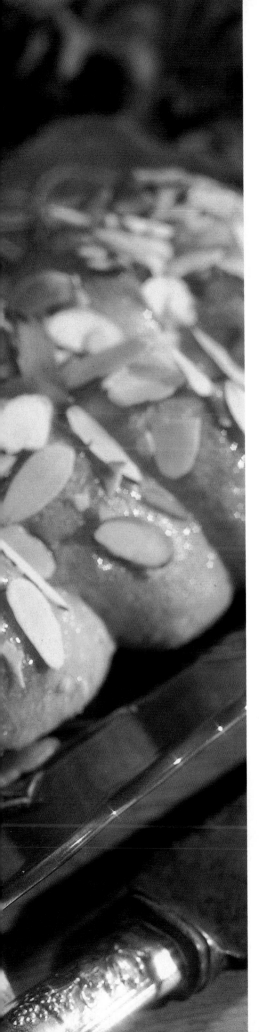

Breads

When you want steaming hot bread for dinner, you don't have to spend all day in the kitchen kneading, rolling, shaping, and waiting for the dough to rise.

Just do what I do—keep at least four quick-fix bread products on hand: reduced-fat biscuit and baking mix, frozen bread dough, refrigerated French bread dough, and hot roll mix. With a pinch of this and a dab of that, you can have fresh bread on the table for dinner in minutes. Why knead, roll, and shape when you can unroll, cut, and bake?

Honey-Almond French Braid (page 50)

It's easy to make your own cinnamon sugar—combine ¼ cup sugar and 1½ teaspoons ground cinnamon.

Orange Gingerbread Muffins

Prep: 10 minutes   Cook: 12 minutes

2 cups reduced-fat biscuit and baking mix (such as Bisquick)
¼ cup cinnamon sugar, divided
½ teaspoon ground ginger
⅔ cup skim milk
¼ cup molasses
1 egg, lightly beaten
1 tablespoon grated orange rind
Butter-flavored vegetable cooking spray

1 Combine baking mix, 3½ tablespoons cinnamon sugar, and ginger in a bowl; make a well in center of mixture. Combine milk and next 3 ingredients, stirring well. Add milk mixture to dry ingredients, stirring just until dry ingredients are moistened.

2 Spoon batter into muffin pans coated with cooking spray, filling one-half full; sprinkle remaining 1½ teaspoons cinnamon sugar over batter. Bake at 400° for 12 minutes. Remove from pans immediately. **Yield: 1 dozen.**

Per Muffin: Calories 122 (14% from fat) Fat 2.0g (Sat 0.4g) Protein 2.5g Carbohydrate 24.0g Fiber 0.3g Cholesterol 19mg Sodium 247mg

Use a slotted spatula to remove the bread slices from the egg substitute mixture. No mess. No stress.

Cinnamon French Toast

Prep: 3 minutes   Cook: 15 minutes

½ cup egg substitute
½ cup skim milk
½ to ¾ teaspoon ground cinnamon
Vegetable cooking spray
1 tablespoon plus 1 teaspoon reduced-calorie margarine, divided
4 (1⅓-ounce) slices honey-wheatberry bread or whole wheat bread

1 Combine first 3 ingredients in a shallow bowl, stirring well with a wire whisk.

2 Coat a nonstick skillet with cooking spray. Add 1 teaspoon margarine; place over medium heat until margarine melts. Dip 1 bread slice into egg substitute mixture. Place coated bread in skillet; cook until browned and crisp on each side, turning once. Repeat with remaining margarine, bread, and egg substitute mixture. **Yield: 4 servings.**

Per Serving: Calories 141 (28% from fat) Fat 4.4g (Sat 0.4g) Protein 7.1g Carbohydrate 21.2g Fiber 3.1g Cholesterol 1mg Sodium 248mg

Yogurt-Pecan Waffles

Prep: 12 minutes   Cook: 8 minutes

1 cup all-purpose flour
1 teaspoon baking powder
½ teaspoon baking soda
¼ teaspoon salt
1 cup plus 2 tablespoons plain nonfat yogurt
¼ cup egg substitute
2 tablespoons reduced-calorie margarine, melted
2 tablespoons finely chopped pecans, toasted
Vegetable cooking spray

1 Combine first 4 ingredients in a medium bowl. Combine yogurt, egg substitute, and margarine; add to dry ingredients, beating well at medium speed of an electric mixer. Stir in pecans.

2 Coat an 8-inch waffle iron with cooking spray; allow waffle iron to preheat. For each waffle, pour 1 cup batter onto hot waffle iron, spreading batter to edges. Bake 4 to 5 minutes or until steaming stops. Cut each waffle into 4 squares.
Yield: 8 (4-inch) waffles.

Per Waffle: Calories 112 (31% from fat)   Fat 3.9g (Sat 0.2g)   Protein 4.4g
Carbohydrate 15.1g   Fiber 0.6g   Cholesterol 1mg   Sodium 215mg

■ Toast pecans in the microwave oven at HIGH 2 to 4 minutes or in the oven at 350° for about 5 minutes.

Yogurt-Pecan Waffles

Drizzle maple syrup over a stack of these slightly sweet pancakes, and the kids will come running to breakfast.

Applesauce Pancakes

Prep: 6 minutes   Cook: 10 minutes

1 cup all-purpose flour
1 teaspoon baking soda
⅛ teaspoon salt
2 tablespoons toasted wheat germ
1 cup nonfat buttermilk
¼ cup applesauce
2 teaspoons vegetable oil
1 egg, lightly beaten
Vegetable cooking spray
Reduced-calorie maple syrup (optional)
Fresh fruit slices (optional)

1 Combine first 4 ingredients in a medium bowl; make a well in center of mixture. Combine buttermilk and next 3 ingredients. Add buttermilk mixture to dry ingredients, stirring just until dry ingredients are moistened.

2 Coat a nonstick griddle or nonstick skillet with cooking spray, and preheat to 350°. For each pancake, pour ¼ cup batter onto hot griddle, spreading to a 5-inch circle. Cook pancakes until tops are covered with bubbles and edges look cooked; turn pancakes, and cook other side. If desired, serve with maple syrup and fresh fruit slices.

Yield: 10 (5-inch) pancakes.

Per Pancake: Calories 81 (20% from fat)   Fat 1.8g (Sat 0.4g)   Protein 3.2g
Carbohydrate 12.8g   Fiber 0.6g   Cholesterol 23mg   Sodium 187mg

Applesauce Pancakes

Tying the Knot

Roll dough into an 8-inch rope.

Cross 1 end of the rope over the other end; then loop the first end through the circle like you're tying a knot.

Italian Biscuit Knots

Prep: 12 minutes   Cook: 12 minutes

2 cups plus 2 tablespoons reduced-fat biscuit and baking mix
      (such as Bisquick), divided
1½ teaspoons dried Italian seasoning
¾ cup skim milk
1 tablespoon fat-free Italian dressing

1 Combine 2 cups baking mix and Italian seasoning, stirring well. Add milk; stir with a fork just until dry ingredients are moistened.

2 Sprinkle remaining 2 tablespoons baking mix evenly over work surface. Turn dough out onto floured surface. Divide dough into 12 equal portions. (Dough will be very soft.) Roll each portion of dough into an 8-inch rope; tie each rope into a loose knot. Place knots on a baking sheet. Brush Italian dressing evenly over biscuits. Bake at 400° for 12 minutes.
Yield: 1 dozen.

Per Biscuit: Calories 87 (14% from fat)   Fat 1.4g (Sat 0.3g)   Protein 2.2g   Carbohydrate 16.1g   Fiber 0.3g   Cholesterol 0mg   Sodium 267mg

Cheddar Drop Biscuits

Prep: 6 minutes   Cook: 8 minutes

2 cups reduced-fat biscuit and baking mix (such as Bisquick)
½ cup (2 ounces) shredded reduced-fat sharp Cheddar cheese
¾ cup skim milk
Vegetable cooking spray
2 tablespoons reduced-calorie margarine, melted
¼ teaspoon garlic powder
½ teaspoon dried parsley flakes, crushed

1 Combine baking mix and cheese in a bowl; make a well in center of mixture. Add milk, stirring just until dry ingredients are moistened.

2 Drop dough by rounded tablespoonfuls, 2 inches apart, onto a baking sheet coated with cooking spray. Bake at 450° for 8 to 10 minutes or until biscuits are golden.

3 Combine margarine, garlic powder, and parsley flakes; brush over warm biscuits. Serve immediately.
Yield: 1 dozen.   *(Biscuits pictured on page 20.)*

Per Biscuit: Calories 106 (30% from fat)   Fat 3.5g (Sat 1.0g)   Protein 3.4g   Carbohydrate 15.0g   Fiber 0.3g   Cholesterol 3mg   Sodium 291mg

Popovers

Prep: 5 minutes   Cook: 50 minutes

1 cup bread flour
1 cup 1% low-fat milk
¾ cup egg substitute
1 tablespoon sugar
1 tablespoon vegetable oil
¼ teaspoon salt
Vegetable cooking spray

1 Position knife blade in food processor bowl; add first 6 ingredients. Process until smooth, stopping once to scrape down sides.

2 Pour batter into popover pans coated with cooking spray, filling one-half full. Place in a cold oven. Turn oven on 450°, and bake 15 minutes. Reduce heat to 350°, and bake 35 to 40 additional minutes or until popovers are crusty and brown.
Yield: 8 popovers.

Per Popover: Calories 109 (21% from fat)   Fat 2.5g (Sat 0.6g)   Protein 5.3g
Carbohydrate 15.9g   Fiber 0.4g   Cholesterol 1mg   Sodium 123mg

■ ■ ■

Orange Popovers: Add 1 tablespoon unsweetened orange juice and 2 teaspoons grated orange rind to flour mixture. Proceed with recipe as directed.

Per Popover: Calories 110 (20% from fat)   Fat 2.5g (Sat 0.6g)   Protein 5.3g
Carbohydrate 16.1g   Fiber 0.4g   Cholesterol 1mg   Sodium 123mg

■ ■ ■

Savory Dillweed Popovers: Add ½ teaspoon dried dillweed and ⅛ teaspoon onion powder to flour mixture. Proceed with recipe as directed.

Per Popover: Calories 109 (21% from fat)   Fat 2.5g (Sat 0.6g)   Protein 5.3g
Carbohydrate 15.9g   Fiber 0.4g   Cholesterol 1mg   Sodium 123mg

■ If you don't have any popover pans, use 8 (6-ounce) ovenproof custard cups.

To make an extra pan of cornbread to freeze and have on hand for later, use the whole package of broccoli and double the rest of the ingredients.

Broccoli Cornbread
Prep: 15 minutes   Cook: 25 minutes

Vegetable cooking spray
1 tablespoon reduced-calorie margarine
½ (10-ounce) package frozen chopped broccoli, thawed and drained
1 (8½-ounce) package corn muffin mix
¾ cup 1% low-fat cottage cheese
½ cup egg substitute
½ cup finely chopped onion
1 (2-ounce) jar diced pimiento, drained
¼ teaspoon cracked pepper

1 Coat an 8-inch square pan with cooking spray. Add margarine, and place in a 350° oven for 3 minutes or until margarine melts.

2 Press broccoli between paper towels to remove excess moisture. Combine broccoli, muffin mix and remaining 5 ingredients, stirring well. Spoon into prepared pan. Bake at 425° for 25 minutes or until golden. **Yield: 16 servings.**

Per Serving: Calories 82 (24% from fat)   Fat 2.2g (Sat 0.7g)   Protein 3.4g   Carbohydrate 12.2g   Fiber 0.9g   Cholesterol 0mg   Sodium 186mg

Broccoli Cornbread

Caraway-Swiss Casserole Bread

Prep: 10 minutes   Rise: 30 minutes   Cook: 45 minutes

1 (16-ounce) package hot roll mix
1⅓ cups warm water (105° to 115°)
1 cup (4 ounces) shredded reduced-fat Swiss cheese
¼ cup finely chopped onion
2 tablespoons margarine, melted
1 tablespoon caraway seeds
1 teaspoon cracked pepper
Vegetable cooking spray

1 Combine yeast packet from roll mix and warm water in a large bowl. Let stand 5 minutes. Add three-fourths of flour packet from roll mix, cheese, and next 4 ingredients. Beat at low speed of an electric mixer until blended. Stir in remaining flour from roll mix.

2 Scrape dough from sides of bowl. Cover and let rise in a warm place (85°), free from drafts, 30 minutes or until doubled in bulk. Stir dough 25 strokes.

3 Coat a 2-quart casserole dish with cooking spray. Spoon dough into dish. Bake at 350° for 45 to 50 minutes or until loaf is browned and sounds hollow when tapped.
Yield: 14 servings. *(Bread pictured on page 24.)*

Per Serving: Calories 160 (25% from fat)   Fat 4.4g (Sat 1.1g)   Protein 6.1g   Carbohydrate 23.1g   Fiber 0.7g   Cholesterol 5mg   Sodium 246mg

Casserole bread is one of the easiest kinds of yeast bread to make because it doesn't require kneading or shaping.

A round glass casserole dish works best for this loaf bread, but any 2-quart casserole dish will do.

Braiding Bread

You don't need a floured surface to work with refrigerated bread dough. You can braid it on your countertop or directly on the baking sheet.

Braid the 3 ropes of dough, and pinch the loose ends together to form 1 braided loaf.

Honey-Almond French Braid

Prep: 8 minutes   Cook: 30 minutes

1 (11-ounce) can refrigerated French bread dough
Vegetable cooking spray
2 tablespoons honey
½ teaspoon water
⅛ teaspoon ground ginger
2 tablespoons sliced almonds

1 Unroll dough; cut into 3 equal pieces. Shape each portion into a rope. Place ropes on a baking sheet coated with cooking spray; (do not stretch). Braid ropes; pinch loose ends to seal. Combine honey, water, and ginger, stirring well. Brush braided dough with half of honey mixture.

2 Bake braid at 350° for 20 minutes. Remove from oven; brush with remaining honey mixture. Sprinkle with almonds. Bake 10 additional minutes or until loaf sounds hollow when tapped. Remove from baking sheet immediately. Serve warm.
Yield: 10 servings. *(Recipe pictured on page 40.)*

Per Serving: Calories 97 (17% from fat)   Fat 1.8g (Sat 0.6g)   Protein 3.3g   Carbohydrate 17.3g   Fiber 0.4g   Cholesterol 0mg   Sodium 195mg

■ ■ ■

Sesame-Garlic French Braid: Shape dough as directed above. Omit honey, water, ginger, and almonds. Cut 2 cloves of garlic into thin slices, and insert slices evenly into braid. Brush 1½ tablespoons melted reduced-calorie margarine over braid, and sprinkle with 2 teaspoons sesame seeds. Bake at 350° for 25 minutes or until loaf sounds hollow when tapped. Remove from baking sheet immediately. Serve warm.
Yield: 10 servings.

Per Serving: Calories 86 (23% from fat)   Fat 2.2g (Sat 0.7g)   Protein 3.1g   Carbohydrate 13.7g   Fiber 0.3g   Cholesterol 0mg   Sodium 212mg

Green Chile Pan Rolls

Prep: 15 minutes   Rise: 16 minutes   Cook: 20 minutes

2 (4½-ounce) cans chopped green chiles, divided
1 package rapid-rise yeast
1 tablespoon sugar
¼ cup warm water (105° to 115°)
½ teaspoon salt
⅛ teaspoon ground red pepper
4 cups plus 1 tablespoon all-purpose flour, divided
¼ cup margarine, divided
⅓ cup cold skim milk
Butter-flavored vegetable cooking spray

1 Drain 1 can chiles, and press firmly between paper towels to remove excess moisture; set aside.

2 Combine yeast, sugar, and water in a 1-cup liquid measuring cup; let stand 5 minutes.

3 Position knife blade in food processor bowl. Add remaining 1 can chopped chiles, salt, and red pepper; process until smooth. Add 4 cups flour and 3 tablespoons margarine; process 15 seconds.

4 Add milk to yeast mixture; stir well. Pour yeast mixture through food chute with processor running. Process 30 seconds or until dough forms a ball; process 1 additional minute. Add drained chiles; process 5 seconds. Add remaining 1 tablespoon flour through food chute with processor running; process 5 seconds.

5 Place dough in a large bowl coated with cooking spray, turning to coat top. Cover and let rise in a warm place (85°), free from drafts, 8 minutes.

6 Turn dough out onto work surface, and divide into 24 equal portions. Shape each portion into a ball. Place balls in two 8-inch round cakepans coated with cooking spray. Cover and let rise in a warm place, free from drafts, 8 minutes. (Rolls will rise slightly.)

7 Melt remaining 1 tablespoon margarine; brush half of melted margarine over tops of rolls. Bake at 375° for 20 minutes or until golden. Remove rolls from pans, and brush with remaining melted margarine.
Yield: 2 dozen.

Per Roll: Calories 101 (20% from fat)   Fat 2.2g (Sat 0.4g)   Protein 2.5g
Carbohydrate 17.6g   Fiber 0.8g   Cholesterol 0mg   Sodium 109mg

Let your food processor take the work out of kneading the dough for these rolls.

What's lazy about yeast rolls, you ask? Make this dough on the weekend, keep it in the refrigerator, and have home-made fresh rolls all week. (These rolls are so yummy that they probably won't last a week.)

Frozen Assets

Invest a little time and get a lot of dough. Make a batch of yeast roll dough to keep in the freezer; then you'll have bread whenever you need it.

Shape the dough into balls as directed.

Freeze the balls on a baking sheet; then put in a zip-top plastic bag and freeze up to 1 month.

To bake, put 12 frozen balls in a cakepan; cover and thaw at room temperature 45 minutes or in refrigerator 8 hours. Let rise, and bake as directed.

Refrigerator Yeast Rolls

**Prep: 20 minutes   Chill: 8 hours   Rise: 45 minutes
Bake: 10 minutes**

1 package active dry yeast
¼ cup warm water (105° to 115°)
¼ cup plus 2 tablespoons sugar, divided
1¾ cups skim milk
¼ cup vegetable oil
1½ teaspoons salt
6 cups plus 1 tablespoon bread flour, divided
Butter-flavored vegetable cooking spray

1 Combine yeast, warm water, and 1 teaspoon sugar in a 1-cup liquid measuring cup; let stand 5 minutes. Combine remaining sugar, milk, oil, and salt in a small saucepan; cook over medium heat until sugar dissolves, stirring occasionally. Cool to 115°. Add yeast mixture to milk mixture, stirring well with a wire whisk.

2 Place 6 cups flour in a large bowl. Gradually add liquid mixture to flour, stirring to make a stiff dough. Place dough in a large bowl coated with cooking spray, turning to coat top. Let stand at room temperature 10 minutes. Cover and refrigerate at least 8 hours. (Dough may remain in refrigerator up to 5 days.)

3 To make rolls, sprinkle remaining 1 tablespoon flour over work surface. Punch dough down; turn out onto floured surface, and knead 2 or 3 times. Divide dough into thirds. Working with 1 portion at a time, shape dough into 12 balls. Place balls in a 9-inch round cakepan coated with cooking spray. Repeat procedure with remaining portions of dough.

4 Cover and let rise in a warm place (85°), free from drafts, 45 minutes or until doubled in bulk. Bake at 400° for 10 to 12 minutes or until golden. Coat rolls lightly with cooking spray.
Yield: 3 dozen.

Per Roll: Calories 111 (17% from fat)   Fat 2.1g (Sat 0.4g)   Protein 3.2g
Carbohydrate 19.5g   Fiber 0.6g   Cholesterol 0mg   Sodium 104mg

Refrigerator Yeast Rolls

Desserts

When I make a dessert, I want it to be delicious, beautiful, sinfully sweet, and of course, low fat. The words time-consuming and challenging are not on my list. Nor should they be on yours.

With a little know-how and products like low-fat cake mixes, ready-made pie crusts, nonfat ice cream, and fresh fruit, I've created the most wonderful treats with the greatest of ease. And even more amazing, I never use more than 7 ingredients.

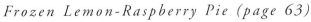

Frozen Lemon-Raspberry Pie (page 63)

Next time you're craving a fruit pie, try a crumble. Instead of rolling pastry dough for a crust, just combine the topping ingredients and sprinkle them over canned fruit.

Pear-Cranberry Crumble

Prep: 10 minutes   Cook: 40 minutes

2 (16-ounce) cans pear halves in light syrup
½ cup dried cranberries
¼ cup plus 1 tablespoon all-purpose flour, divided
½ teaspoon ground allspice
Vegetable cooking spray
⅔ cup quick-cooking oats, uncooked
¼ cup firmly packed brown sugar
¼ cup reduced-calorie stick margarine

1 Drain pears, reserving ¾ cup liquid. Discard remaining liquid. Combine pears, ¾ cup liquid, and cranberries. Combine 1 tablespoon flour and allspice; sprinkle over pear mixture, and toss lightly. Spoon mixture into an 8-inch square pan coated with cooking spray.

2 Combine remaining ¼ cup flour, oats, and sugar. Cut in margarine with a pastry blender until mixture resembles coarse meal. Sprinkle oat mixture over pear mixture. Bake at 375° for 40 minutes. **Yield: 8 servings.**

Per Serving: Calories 170 (23% from fat)   Fat 4.3g (Sat 0.6g)   Protein 1.8g   Carbohydrate 33.3g   Fiber 3.6g   Cholesterol 0mg   Sodium 62mg

To keep this dessert low in fat, read the nutrition labels to find refrigerated biscuits with no more than 2.5 grams of fat per biscuit.

Oven-Fried Peach Pies

Prep: 15 minutes   Bake: 10 minutes

1 cup drained canned peaches in light syrup, chopped
3 tablespoons sugar, divided
¾ teaspoon ground cinnamon, divided
1 tablespoon all-purpose flour
1 (10-ounce) can refrigerated buttermilk biscuits
Butter-flavored vegetable cooking spray

1 Combine peaches, 2 tablespoons sugar, and ½ teaspoon cinnamon. Sprinkle flour over work surface. Separate biscuits; place on floured surface. Roll each biscuit to a 4½-inch circle. Place one heaping tablespoon peach mixture over half of each circle. Brush edges of circles with water; fold in half. Seal edges by pressing with a fork.

2 Place pies on a ungreased baking sheet; coat with cooking spray. Combine remaining 1 tablespoon sugar and ¼ teaspoon cinnamon; sprinkle over pies. Bake at 375° for 10 minutes. **Yield: 10 pies.**

Per Pie: Calories 107 (22% from fat)   Fat 2.6g (Sat 1.0g)   Protein 2.2g   Carbohydrate 19.9g   Fiber 0.4g   Cholesterol 0mg   Sodium 281mg

Apple Turnovers

Prep: 20 minutes   Bake: 15 minutes

1 cup chopped reduced-calorie apple pie filling
¼ cup raisins
½ teaspoon apple pie spice
6 sheets frozen phyllo pastry, thawed
Butter-flavored vegetable cooking spray
1 cup sifted powdered sugar
1 tablespoon plus 1 teaspoon 1% low-fat milk

1 Combine first 3 ingredients in a small bowl; set aside.

2 Place 1 sheet of phyllo on a damp towel (keep remaining phyllo covered). Lightly coat phyllo with cooking spray. Place another sheet of phyllo over first sheet; coat with cooking spray. Cut stacked sheets lengthwise into 4 equal strips (each about 3¼ inches wide).

3 Working with one strip at a time, place 1 heaping tablespoon apple mixture at base of strip (keep remaining strips covered). Fold the right bottom corner over apple mixture to form a triangle. Continue folding the triangle back and forth to end of strip. Repeat folding process with next 3 strips. Place triangles, seam sides down, on a baking sheet coated with cooking spray. (Keep triangles covered before baking.) Repeat procedure twice with remaining phyllo sheets and apple mixture.

4 Bake at 400° for 15 minutes or until golden. Remove from baking sheet, and let cool 5 minutes on a wire rack. Combine powdered sugar and milk, stirring until smooth. Drizzle sugar mixture evenly over turnovers. Serve warm.
Yield: 12 turnovers.

Per Turnover: Calories 108 (9% from fat) Fat 1.1g (Sat 0.1g) Protein 1.2g
Carbohydrate 23.6g Fiber 0.4g Cholesterol 0mg Sodium 72mg

Turn Out a Turnover

Cut the stacked sheets of phyllo into lengthwise strips. Use a ruler to help you cut straight strips.

Place 1 heaping tablespoon of filling at the base of each strip.

Fold the right bottom corner of the strip over the filling to form a triangle.

Fold the triangle back and forth to the end of the strip.

■ Tiramisù is an Italian dessert with layers of coffee liqueur-soaked spongecake, mascarpone (a sweet cream cheese), and chocolate.

Tiramisù

Prep: 25 minutes

½ cup plus 1 tablespoon Kahlúa or other coffee-flavored liqueur
¼ cup plus 1 tablespoon sugar, divided
2 tablespoons water
1 tablespoon plus 1 teaspoon instant espresso powder
¼ cup plus 2 tablespoons liquid fat-free hazelnut-flavored
    nondairy coffee creamer
1 cup light process cream cheese, softened
1½ cups frozen reduced-calorie whipped topping, thawed
1 (13.6-ounce) loaf fat-free pound cake, cut into 16 slices
Unsweetened cocoa (optional)

1 Combine liqueur, 1 tablespoon sugar, water, and espresso powder, stirring until sugar and espresso powder dissolve. Spoon 2 tablespoons mixture into a medium bowl; set remaining mixture aside.

2 Add remaining ¼ cup sugar and creamer to 2 tablespoons liqueur mixture in bowl, stirring until sugar dissolves. Add cream cheese; beat at medium speed of an electric mixer until smooth. Fold in whipped topping.

3 Place 1 cake slice in each of 8 wine glasses or 8 (4-ounce) custard cups. Brush cake in glasses generously with half of reserved liqueur mixture. Spread cheese mixture evenly over cake. Top with remaining 8 cake slices. Gently press slices into glasses. Brush cake with remaining liqueur mixture. Sprinkle evenly with cocoa, if desired. Serve immediately.
Yield: 8 servings.

Per Serving: Calories 323 (18% from fat)   Fat 6.4g (Sat 3.7g)   Protein 6.3g
Carbohydrate 50.3g   Fiber 0.3g   Cholesterol 16mg   Sodium 924mg

Tiramisù

Instant pudding mix is a quick alternative to custard filling in layered desserts like trifle.

Creamy Citrus Trifle

Prep: 20 minutes   Chill: 3 hours

1 (3.4-ounce) package lemon instant pudding mix
2 cups skim milk
1 (8-ounce) carton low-fat sour cream
⅓ cup low-sugar orange marmalade
1 tablespoon dry sherry
8 ounces angel food cake, cut into ¾-inch cubes
2 (11-ounce) cans mandarin oranges in light syrup, drained

1 Combine pudding mix and skim milk, stirring until smooth. Stir in sour cream; set aside. Combine marmalade and sherry, stirring with a wire whisk until blended.

2 Arrange half of cake cubes in a 1½-quart trifle bowl or straight-sided glass bowl. Spoon half of pudding mixture over cake. Drizzle marmalade mixture over pudding mixture. Arrange half of oranges over marmalade mixture. Repeat layers with remaining cake, pudding mixture, and oranges. Cover and chill at least 3 hours.
Yield: 8 servings.

Per Serving: Calories 197 (16% from fat)   Fat 3.6g (Sat 2.2g)   Protein 4.7g
Carbohydrate 37.2g   Fiber 0.0g   Cholesterol 12mg   Sodium 341mg

You may want to vary the frozen fruit in this simple four-ingredient ice cream. Try peaches, strawberries, or blackberries.

Raspberry-Almond Ice Cream

Prep: 5 minutes   Freeze: 15 minutes   Stand: 2 hours

1 (14-ounce) can low-fat sweetened condensed milk
2 cups 1% low-fat milk
1 (10-ounce) package frozen raspberries in syrup, thawed
½ teaspoon almond extract

1 Combine all ingredients, stirring until blended. Pour milk mixture into freezer can of a 2-quart hand-turned or electric freezer. Freeze according to manufacturer's instructions. Pack freezer with additional ice and rock salt, and let stand 2 hours before serving.
Yield: 10 (½-cup) servings.

Per Serving: Calories 159 (11% from fat)   Fat 2.0g (Sat 1.3g)   Protein 2.0g
Carbohydrate 29.7g   Fiber 1.0g   Cholesterol 7mg   Sodium 65mg

Rocky Road Ice Cream

Prep: 10 minutes   Freeze: 10 minutes   Stand: 1 hour

1 (3.9-ounce) package chocolate instant pudding mix
2 tablespoons sugar
1 cup skim milk
1 (12-ounce) can evaporated skimmed milk
¾ cup miniature marshmallows
½ cup semisweet chocolate mini-morsels
¼ cup coarsely chopped unsalted dry roasted peanuts

1 Combine pudding mix and sugar in a large bowl. Gradually add skim milk and evaporated milk, stirring with a wire whisk until smooth. Stir in marshmallows, chocolate morsels, and peanuts.

2 Pour chocolate mixture into freezer can of a 2-quart hand-turned or electric freezer. Freeze according to manufacturer's instructions. Pack freezer with additional ice and rock salt, and let stand at least 1 hour before serving.
Yield: 8 (½-cup) servings.

Per Serving: Calories 203 (27% from fat)   Fat 6.2g (Sat 2.5g)   Protein 6.0g
Carbohydrate 33.2g   Fiber 1.0g   Cholesterol 2mg   Sodium 273mg

■ The combination of pudding mix and evaporated milk gives this frozen dessert a creamy texture with no added fat. The chocolate morsels and the peanuts add a little crunch.

Rocky Road
Ice Cream

A Cupful of Cookie

Commercial fat-free oatmeal-raisin cookies make ideal dessert cups. The cookies are soft enough to press into muffin cups, and they retain the cup shape when removed from the muffin pans.

Place 1 cookie in each muffin cup, pressing the cookie into the cup to make a shell.

Peachy Ice Cream Desserts

Prep: 20 minutes   Freeze: 2 hours

2½ cups light cheesecake chunk ice cream, softened
1½ cups sliced frozen peaches, thawed and coarsely chopped
2 teaspoons lemon juice
½ cup no-sugar-added peach spread
¼ cup amaretto, divided
1 (11-ounce) package fat-free soft oatmeal-raisin cookies (such as Archway)

1 Combine first 3 ingredients. Spread ice cream mixture into an 8-inch square pan. Cover and freeze 2 hours or until firm.

2 Combine peach spread and 2 tablespoons amaretto in a small saucepan. Cook over low heat, stirring constantly, until peach spread melts; set aside, and keep warm.

3 Place 1 cookie in each of 10 (2½-inch) muffin cups. Firmly press cookies against bottoms and up sides of cups. Brush cookies evenly with remaining 2 tablespoons amaretto; let stand 15 minutes.

4 Remove cookie cups from pan, and place on individual dessert plates. Scoop ice cream mixture into cookie cups. Drizzle evenly with peach spread mixture.
Yield: 10 servings.

Per Serving: Calories 222 (10% from fat)   Fat 2.5g (Sat 1.5g)   Protein 2.7g   Carbohydrate 43.6g   Fiber 1.4g   Cholesterol 13mg   Sodium 188mg

Praline-Chocolate Bombe

Prep: 15 minutes   Freeze: 8 hours

1 cup reduced-fat gingersnap cookie crumbs (about 25 cookies)
2 tablespoons reduced-calorie margarine, melted
4 cups low-fat praline and caramel ice cream, softened
2¾ ounces commercial fat-free brownies, cut into cubes
¼ cup finely chopped pecans, toasted
¼ cup fat-free caramel-flavored syrup
½ cup plus 2 tablespoons praline liqueur

1 Line a 1½-quart bowl with heavy-duty plastic wrap. Combine crumbs and margarine; press into bottom and up sides of bowl, leaving a 1-inch space around top of bowl. Combine ice cream and next 3 ingredients; spoon into bowl. Cover and freeze at least 8 hours.

2 To serve, let stand at room temperature 5 minutes. Invert onto a serving plate; remove bowl and plastic wrap. Cut into wedges. Drizzle 1 tablespoon liqueur over each wedge. Serve immediately.
Yield: 10 servings.

Per Serving: Calories 249 (25% from fat)   Fat 6.8g (Sat 1.3g)   Protein 3.6g
Carbohydrate 43.8g   Fiber 0.7g   Cholesterol 2mg   Sodium 171mg

■ If you prefer not to use praline liqueur, drizzle each wedge with 2 teaspoons fat-free caramel-flavored syrup.

Frozen Lemon-Raspberry Pie

Prep: 15 minutes   Freeze: 2 hours and 15 minutes

1¾ cups reduced-fat gingersnap cookie crumbs (about 40 cookies)
3 tablespoons reduced-calorie margarine, melted
2 tablespoons minced crystallized ginger
4 cups raspberry sorbet, softened
4 cups lemon sorbet, softened
3 cups fresh raspberries
3 (1-ounce) squares white chocolate, melted
Fresh mint sprigs (optional)

1 Combine first 3 ingredients, stirring well. Press into bottom of a 10-inch springform pan; freeze 15 minutes or until firm. Spread raspberry sorbet over crumb mixture. Freeze 1 hour. Spread lemon sorbet over raspberry sorbet. Cover and freeze 1 hour.

2 To serve, remove pie from pan. Arrange raspberries over lemon sorbet. Drizzle white chocolate over raspberries; slice pie into wedges. Garnish with mint sprigs, if desired.
Yield: 12 servings. *(Recipe pictured on page 54.)*

Per Serving: Calories 312 (23% from fat)   Fat 7.8g (Sat 3.2g)   Protein 2.7g
Carbohydrate 58.4g   Fiber 2.7g   Cholesterol 8mg   Sodium 145mg

■ For an easy way to drizzle the white chocolate over the pie, place the chocolate in a heavy-duty, zip-top plastic bag and microwave at LOW for 1 minute. Snip a hole in one bottom corner of the bag, and squeeze.

Malibu Brownie Torte

Malibu Brownie Torte

Prep: 15 minutes   Cook: 20 minutes   Freeze: 2 hours

½ (20.5-ounce) package low-fat fudge brownie mix (such as
    Sweet Rewards)
⅓ cup water
Vegetable cooking spray
¾ cup fat-free fudge topping, divided
6 cups fat-free vanilla ice cream, softened
¼ cup semisweet chocolate mini-morsels
¼ cup Malibu rum (or ¼ cup rum and ½ teaspoon coconut
    extract)
1½ tablespoons flaked coconut, toasted
Strawberry fans (optional)

1 Combine ½ package brownie mix and ⅓ cup water, stirring just
until dry ingredients are moistened. Reserve remaining brownie mix
for another use. Pour batter into a 9-inch springform pan coated
with cooking spray. Bake at 350° for 18 to 20 minutes or until edges
pull away from pan slightly. Let cool in pan on a wire rack. Spread ½
cup fudge topping over brownie.

2 Combine ice cream, chocolate morsels, and rum in a large bowl,
stirring well. Spread ice cream mixture over brownie. Freeze 2 hours
or until firm.

3 To serve, remove torte from pan. Drizzle remaining ¼ cup fudge
topping over torte. Sprinkle with coconut. Garnish each slice with a
strawberry fan, if desired.
Yield: 12 servings.

Per Serving: Calories 275 (11% from fat)   Fat 3.4g (Sat 1.4g)   Protein 5.0g
Carbohydrate 56.5g   Fiber 2.3g   Cholesterol 0mg   Sodium 154mg

■ Desserts just don't get much better than this layered frozen pie. It's got a fudgy brownie crust and a chocolate chip ice cream filling with coconut and fudge sauce on top. All this and low fat, too!

So you won't miss out on a single bite, coat each paper liner with cooking spray; then the fudgy cupcake won't stick to the paper.

Chocolate Cream Cupcakes

Prep: 15 minutes   Cook: 25 minutes

1 (20.5-ounce) package low-fat fudge brownie mix
⅔ cup water
Vegetable cooking spray
2 ounces Neufchâtel cheese, softened
1½ tablespoons sugar
1 tablespoon semisweet chocolate morsels, melted

1 Combine brownie mix and water; stir until blended. Reserve ¾ cup batter. Spoon remaining batter evenly into 12 muffin cups lined with paper liners coated with cooking spray.

2 Combine cheese and sugar, stirring well until creamy. Stir in melted chocolate. Spoon 1 teaspoon cheese mixture into center of each cupcake. Top evenly with remaining batter (about 1 tablespoon per muffin cup). Bake at 350° for 25 minutes. Cool in pan 5 minutes. Remove from pan, and let cool completely on a wire rack. **Yield: 1 dozen.**

Per Cupcake: Calories 219 (21% from fat)   Fat 5.1g (Sat 2.3g)   Protein 3.5g   Carbohydrate 43.1g   Fiber 1.5g   Cholesterol 3mg   Sodium 194mg

This easy recipe turns a commercial pound cake loaf into a frosted fruit-filled layer cake.

Orange-Pineapple Fluff Cake

Prep: 15 minutes   Chill: 1 hour

1 (13.6-ounce) loaf commercial fat-free pound cake
¼ cup unsweetened orange juice
2 teaspoons Triple Sec or other orange-flavored liqueur
1 (9-ounce) jar reduced-calorie apricot-pineapple preserves
1 (8-ounce) can crushed pineapple in juice
2½ cups frozen reduced-calorie whipped topping, thawed

1 Punch holes in cake at 1-inch intervals with a wooden pick. Combine orange juice and liqueur; pour over cake. Slice cake horizontally into 4 layers. Place 1 cake layer on a serving plate. Spread one-third of preserves over layer. Repeat procedure with remaining cake layers and preserves, ending with cake layer.

2 Drain pineapple, and press between paper towels to remove excess moisture. Fold pineapple into whipped topping. Spread topping mixture over top and sides of cake. Cover and chill at least 1 hour. **Yield: 8 servings.**

Per Serving: Calories 229 (11% from fat)   Fat 2.8g (Sat 1.4g)   Protein 2.7g   Carbohydrate 45.7g   Fiber 0.8g   Cholesterol 0mg   Sodium 175mg

Chocolate Cream Cupcakes

A cast-iron skillet works best for getting the cake golden and crispy on the outside and tender on the inside.

Pineapple Upside-Down Cake

Prep: 15 minutes   Cook: 35 minutes

⅓ cup reduced-calorie margarine
¾ cup firmly packed brown sugar
⅓ cup chopped pecans
1 (15¼-ounce) can sliced pineapple in juice
½ (18.25-ounce) package reduced-fat yellow cake mix
¼ cup plus 2 tablespoons egg substitute
⅓ cup water
7 maraschino cherries with stems

1 Melt margarine in a 10-inch cast-iron skillet over low heat. Set aside 1 tablespoon margarine. Add sugar and pecans to margarine in skillet, stirring well. Drain pineapple, reserving ⅓ cup juice. Discard remaining juice. Arrange pineapple over sugar mixture.

2 Combine reserved 1 tablespoon margarine, ⅓ cup juice, cake mix, egg substitute, and water. Beat at low speed of an electric mixer 30 seconds. Beat at medium speed 2 minutes. Pour batter over pineapple in skillet. Bake at 350° for 35 minutes or until a wooden pick inserted in center comes out clean. Immediately invert cake onto a serving platter. Place cherries in centers of pineapple rings.
Yield: 10 servings.

Per Serving: Calories 254 (28% from fat)   Fat 8.0g (Sat 1.5g)   Protein 2.3g
Carbohydrate 44.5g   Fiber 0.7g   Cholesterol 0mg   Sodium 244mg

*Pineapple
Upside-Down
Cake*

Banana Cream Pie

Prep: 11 minutes   Cook: 8 minutes   Chill: 1½ hours

1 cup reduced-fat chocolate graham cracker crumbs
      (about 10 crackers)
¼ cup reduced-calorie margarine, melted
1 (3.4-ounce) package banana cream-flavored instant pudding mix
1 cup 1% low-fat milk
¼ cup plus 1 tablespoon crème de cacao or other chocolate-
      flavored liqueur, divided
1¾ cups frozen reduced-calorie whipped topping, thawed and
      divided
1¼ cups peeled, sliced banana

1 Combine cracker crumbs and margarine, stirring well. Press into bottom and up sides of a 9-inch pieplate. Bake at 350° for 8 minutes. Remove from oven, and let cool on a wire rack.

2 Combine pudding mix, milk, and ¼ cup liqueur in a medium bowl, stirring with a wire whisk until smooth. Gently fold 1 cup whipped topping into pudding mixture.

3 Toss banana slices with remaining 1 tablespoon liqueur, and arrange over prepared crust. Spoon pudding mixture over banana slices. Cover and chill 1½ hours or until set. Pipe or spoon remaining ¾ cup whipped topping around edge of pie just before serving.
Yield: 8 servings.

Per Serving: Calories 268 (28% from fat) Fat 8.4g (Sat 2.1g) Protein 3.3g
Carbohydrate 42.5g Fiber 1.1g Cholesterol 1mg Sodium 400mg

■ For a kid-friendly version of this pie, omit the crème de cacao and increase the milk by ¼ cup. Toss the bananas in 1 tablespoon lemon juice instead of the liqueur.

For a special touch, top each serving with a dollop of reduced-fat whipped topping and sprinkle lightly with pumpkin pie spice.

Sweet Potato Pie

Prep: 10 minutes   Cook: 1 hour and 5 minutes

1 (14½-ounce) can no-sugar-added mashed sweet potatoes
2 tablespoons reduced-calorie margarine
¾ cup firmly packed brown sugar
1 teaspoon pumpkin pie spice
⅓ cup egg substitute
⅓ cup evaporated skimmed milk
1 (6-ounce) reduced-fat graham cracker pie crust

1 Place sweet potato and margarine in a medium-size microwave-safe bowl. Microwave at HIGH 3 minutes or until potato is thoroughly heated; stir well. Add brown sugar and pumpkin pie spice to potato mixture; stir well. Gradually add egg substitute and milk, stirring well. Pour potato mixture into pie crust.

2 Bake at 400° for 10 minutes. Reduce heat to 350°, and bake 55 additional minutes or until set. Let pie cool on a wire rack.
Yield: 8 servings.

Per Serving: Calories 261 (17% from fat)   Fat 5.0g (Sat 1.3g)   Protein 3.7g   Carbohydrate 50.1g   Fiber 2.1g   Cholesterol 0mg   Sodium 165mg

Remove the cookies from the cookie sheets before they cool. They will crumble if you let them cool on the cookie sheets.

Sweet Cornmeal Cookies

Prep: 5 minutes   Stand: 1 hour   Bake: 5 minutes per batch

⅔ cup firmly packed brown sugar
½ cup all-purpose flour
2 tablespoons cornmeal
Dash of salt
¼ cup margarine, melted
2 egg whites, lightly beaten
Vegetable cooking spray

1 Combine first 4 ingredients. Add margarine and egg whites; stir well. Cover and let stand 1 hour. (Batter will be thin.)

2 Spoon batter by level teaspoonfuls, 2 inches apart, onto cookie sheets coated with cooking spray. Bake at 400° for 5 minutes or until edges are browned. Let cool on cookie sheets 1 minute. Remove from cookie sheets. Let cool completely on wire racks.
Yield: 44 cookies.

Per Cookie: Calories 29 (34% from fat)   Fat 1.1g (Sat 0.2g)   Protein 0.3g   Carbohydrate 4.6g   Fiber 0.1g   Cholesterol 0mg   Sodium 19mg

Cinnamon Sugar Cookies

Prep: 24 minutes   Cook: 6 minutes per batch

3   tablespoons reduced-calorie stick margarine, softened
⅔   cup plus 1½ tablespoons sugar, divided
1   egg
1½   teaspoons vanilla extract
1½   cups plus 1½ teaspoons all-purpose flour, divided
½   teaspoon baking soda
½   teaspoon plus ⅛ teaspoon ground cinnamon, divided

1 Beat margarine at medium speed of an electric mixer until creamy; gradually add ⅔ cup sugar, beating well. Add egg and vanilla; beat well. Combine 1½ cups flour, baking soda, and ½ teaspoon cinnamon; gradually add to margarine mixture, beating well.

2 Sprinkle remaining 1½ teaspoons flour evenly over work surface. Turn dough out onto floured surface. Lightly flour hands, and shape dough into 26 balls. Combine remaining 1½ tablespoons sugar and remaining ⅛ teaspoon ground cinnamon. Roll balls in sugar mixture. Place balls, 3 inches apart, on ungreased cookie sheets. Pat each into a 2-inch circle. Bake at 375° for 6 to 8 minutes or until golden. Remove from cookie sheets; let cool completely on wire racks. **Yield: 26 cookies.**

Per Cookie: Calories 60 (17% from fat)   Fat 1.1g (Sat 0.1g)   Protein 1.0g
Carbohydrate 11.4g   Fiber 0.2g   Cholesterol 8mg   Sodium 40mg

■ The cookie dough will be slightly sticky, so it helps to put some flour on your hands as you shape the dough into balls.

Peanut Butter Crunch Cookies

Prep: 12 minutes   Stand: 30 minutes

3   cups corn flakes cereal
½   cup light-colored corn syrup
3   tablespoons sugar
⅓   cup reduced-fat peanut butter spread

1 Place cereal in a large bowl; set aside. Combine syrup and sugar in a saucepan. Bring to a boil over medium-high heat; cook 1 minute. Remove from heat; stir in peanut butter.

2 Working quickly, pour peanut butter mixture over cereal; toss lightly to coat. Drop by heaping tablespoonfuls onto wax paper. Let stand at room temperature until firm. Store in an airtight container. **Yield: 26 cookies.**

Per Cookie: Calories 55 (20% from fat)   Fat 1.2g (Sat 0.2g)   Protein 1.1g
Carbohydrate 10.4g   Fiber 0.1g   Cholesterol 0mg   Sodium 62mg

■ These no-bake treats take less than 15 minutes of effort and are great as after-school snacks.

When you roll the cookies in Grape Nuts cereal before baking, they have a crunchy coating that's like the crunch you get with nuts.

Thumbprint Cookies

Prep: 30 minutes   Cook: 20 minutes per batch

¾ cup reduced-calorie stick margarine, softened
⅔ cup sugar
¼ cup egg substitute
½ teaspoon vanilla, butter, and nut flavoring
2¼ cups all-purpose flour
¼ teaspoon salt
1 cup nutlike cereal nuggets (such as Grape Nuts)
½ cup low-sugar strawberry spread

1 Beat margarine at medium speed of an electric mixer until creamy; gradually add sugar, beating well. Add egg substitute and flavoring; beat well. Combine flour and salt; gradually add to margarine mixture, beating well. Cover dough, and freeze 10 minutes.

2 Shape dough into 48 (1-inch) balls; roll in cereal. Place 2 inches apart on ungreased cookie sheets. Press thumb into each ball to make an indentation. Bake at 300° for 20 minutes. Remove from cookie sheets; let cool on wire racks. Fill each center with ½ teaspoon spread. **Yield: 4 dozen.**

Per Cookie: Calories 59 (29% from fat)   Fat 1.9g (Sat 0.3g)   Protein 1.1g
Carbohydrate 10.1g   Fiber 0.5g   Cholesterol 0mg   Sodium 63mg

It's smart to use your microwave oven to melt the marshmallows. You won't have to stir the marshmallows as they melt, plus they're less likely to burn.

Cappuccino Crispies

Prep: 10 minutes   Cool: 1 hour

1 tablespoon instant coffee granules
1 tablespoon hot water
1 teaspoon vanilla extract
1 (10-ounce) package marshmallows
5 cups crisp rice cereal
Vegetable cooking spray

1 Combine first 3 ingredients, stirring until coffee dissolves.

2 Place marshmallows in a 2-quart glass measure. Microwave at HIGH 1½ to 2 minutes or until marshmallows melt. Remove from microwave; stir until smooth. Add coffee mixture to melted marshmallows; stir well. Working quickly, add cereal to marshmallow mixture, stirring lightly to coat. Press mixture into a 13- x 9- x 2-inch pan coated with cooking spray. Let cool completely. Cut into bars. **Yield: 24 bars.**

Per Bar: Calories 63 (1% from fat)   Fat 0.1g (Sat 0.0g)   Protein 0.6g
Carbohydrate 14.9g   Fiber 0.1g   Cholesterol 0mg   Sodium 49mg

Caramel-Oatmeal Bars

Prep: 8 minutes   Cook: 40 minutes   Chill: 1 hour

1¼ cups quick-cooking oats, uncooked
1¼ cups all-purpose flour, divided
⅔ cup firmly packed brown sugar
½ cup reduced-calorie stick margarine
Vegetable cooking spray
⅓ cup finely chopped walnuts
¾ cup fat-free caramel-flavored syrup

1 Combine oats, 1 cup flour, and sugar in a large bowl. Cut in margarine with a pastry blender until mixture resembles coarse meal. Press one-half of oat mixture into bottom of a 9-inch square pan coated with cooking spray. Bake at 350° for 15 minutes. Remove from oven; sprinkle walnuts over prepared crust.

2 Combine syrup and remaining ¼ cup flour; stir well. Pour syrup mixture over nuts. Sprinkle remaining oat mixture over syrup mixture. Bake at 350° 25 to 30 minutes or until golden. Let cool in pan on a wire rack. Cover and chill at least 1 hour. Cut into bars.
Yield: 24 bars.

Per Bar: Calories 116 (28% from fat)   Fat 3.6g (Sat 0.5g)   Protein 1.9g
Carbohydrate 19.0g   Fiber 0.7g   Cholesterol 0mg   Sodium 43mg

■ Reduced-calorie stick margarine works better than tub margarine in these cookies because the stick margarine is easier to cut into the flour.

Fish ∷ Shellfish

The medical experts give me three good reasons why I should eat more fish. (1) It reduces my chances of getting heart disease. (2) It may prevent cancer. (3) It helps me lose weight. Great! I'm sure that they have all their facts right.

As far as I'm concerned, there are three more excellent reasons to put fish on my menu. (1) It cooks fast. (2) It tastes great. (3) It impresses my dinner guests.

All I have to do is brush a little soy sauce, garlic, and brown sugar on salmon steaks, and my guests think that I had the fish flown in fresh from Alaska.

Glazed Salmon Steaks (page 82)

■ If amberjack are not swimming in your area waters, use another lean, mild fish such as swordfish or mahi mahi.

Fish Market

Use the following list to help you make fish substitutions. Try to select the same form of the fish—whole, fillets, or steaks.

Bass: grouper, halibut, red snapper

Catfish: haddock, pollack, flounder

Flounder: ocean perch, orange roughy, sole, turbot

Haddock: cod, ocean catfish, flounder

Halibut: sea bass, snapper, monkfish

Mackerel: bluefish, lake trout

Perch: walleye pike, orange roughy, flounder, turbot, sole

Pompano: snapper, sea bass, yellowtail, redfish

Redfish: snapper, grouper, halibut

Salmon: swordfish, halibut, lake trout, yellowtail

Snapper: sea bass, grouper, redfish, pompano

Sole: flounder, turbot, orange roughy, ocean perch

Swordfish: halibut, shark, marlin, tuna

Grilled Amberjack with Caramelized Onion

Prep: 9 minutes   Marinate: 30 minutes   Cook: 30 minutes

¼ cup plus 2 tablespoons reduced-calorie maple syrup, divided
3 tablespoons low-sodium teriyaki sauce
1 tablespoon lemon juice
2 teaspoons minced garlic
6 (4-ounce) amberjack fillets (¾ inch thick)
Butter-flavored vegetable cooking spray
1 large sweet onion, thinly sliced
2 teaspoons margarine, melted

1 Combine ¼ cup maple syrup, teriyaki sauce, lemon juice, and garlic in a large heavy-duty, zip-top plastic bag. Add fish. Seal bag, and shake gently until fish is well coated. Marinate in refrigerator 30 minutes.

2 Coat one side of a 12-inch square of heavy-duty aluminum foil with cooking spray. Place onion slices on half of coated side of foil. Combine remaining 2 tablespoons maple syrup and margarine, stirring well. Drizzle syrup mixture over onion. Fold foil over onion; crimp edges to seal.

3 Coat grill rack with cooking spray; place on grill over medium-hot coals (350° to 400°). Place foil packet on rack; grill, covered, 20 to 25 minutes or until onion is tender and golden. Set aside, and keep warm.

4 Remove fish from marinade, reserving marinade. Place marinade in a small saucepan; bring to a boil, and set aside. Place fish on rack; grill, covered, 4 to 6 minutes on each side or until fish flakes easily when tested with a fork, basting often with reserved marinade. Transfer fish to a serving platter; top evenly with onion.
Yield: 6 servings.

Per Serving: Calories 147 (17% from fat)   Fat 2.8g (Sat 0.6g)   Protein 21.5g
Carbohydrate 8.6g   Fiber 1.0g   Cholesterol 58mg   Sodium 270mg

Cajun-Spiced Catfish

Prep: 5 minutes   Cook: 7 minutes

2 tablespoons reduced-calorie margarine, melted
1 teaspoon dried basil
1 teaspoon dried thyme
1 teaspoon paprika
1 teaspoon black pepper
1 teaspoon ground red pepper
½ teaspoon salt
⅛ teaspoon garlic powder
4 (4-ounce) farm-raised catfish fillets
Vegetable cooking spray

1 Combine first 8 ingredients in a small bowl.

2 Place fish on rack of a broiler pan coated with cooking spray. Brush fish with margarine mixture. Broil 5½ inches from heat (with electric oven door partially opened) 7 minutes or until fish flakes easily when tested with a fork.
Yield: 4 servings.   *(Fish pictured on page 20.)*

Per Serving: Calories 170 (47% from fat)   Fat 8.8g (Sat 1.7g)   Protein 20.9g
Carbohydrate 1.4g   Fiber 0.5g   Cholesterol 66mg   Sodium 420mg

■ This quick recipe is a great alternative to blackened fish. The fish has the same spicy flavor without the hassle of blackening the fillets in an iron skillet.

Greek-Style Flounder

Prep: 7 minutes   Cook: 15 minutes

¼ cup lemon juice
1½ tablespoons balsamic vinegar
1 teaspoon dried oregano
1½ teaspoons olive oil
¼ teaspoon salt
⅛ teaspoon pepper
4 (4-ounce) flounder fillets
Vegetable cooking spray
3 tablespoons chopped fresh parsley

1 Combine first 6 ingredients in a small bowl.

2 Place fish in a 13- x 9- x 2-inch baking dish coated with cooking spray; pour lemon juice mixture over fish. Bake at 350° for 13 to 15 minutes or until fish flakes easily when tested with a fork. Sprinkle with parsley.
Yield: 4 servings.

Per Serving: Calories 115 (19% from fat)   Fat 2.4g (Sat 0.4g)   Protein 21.5g
Carbohydrate 0.9g   Fiber 0.1g   Cholesterol 54mg   Sodium 166mg

■ Don't throw away the herbed lemon cooking liquid from the fish. Instead, spoon it over cooked rice for a savory side dish.

Recapture the days of scout campouts and grilling your dinner in a foil packet over an open fire. No kindling required—you bake this dish in the oven.

Hobo Fish Dinner

Prep: 15 minutes   Cook: 30 minutes

Vegetable cooking spray
1 teaspoon salt-free lemon-pepper seasoning
½ teaspoon salt
½ teaspoon dried dillweed
4 small baking potatoes, thinly sliced
3 cups thinly sliced onion (about 2 medium)
1 cup thinly sliced carrot (about 2 medium)
4 (4-ounce) halibut fillets (or any firm white fish)

1 Coat one side of 4 (18-inch) squares of heavy-duty aluminum foil with cooking spray.

2 Combine lemon-pepper seasoning, salt, and dillweed. Arrange potato slices evenly in centers of coated foil squares. Sprinkle potato with one-third of seasoning mixture. Place onion over potato; sprinkle with one-half of remaining seasoning mixture. Top with carrot slices, and sprinkle with remaining seasoning mixture. Place fish over vegetables. Fold foil over fish and vegetables; crimp edges to seal.

3 Place foil packets on a baking sheet. Bake at 450° for 30 to 35 minutes or until fish flakes easily when tested with a fork.
Yield: 4 servings.

Per Serving: Calories 268 (11% from fat)   Fat 3.2g (Sat 0.4g)   Protein 27.8g   Carbohydrate 32.0g   Fiber 5.1g   Cholesterol 53mg   Sodium 378mg

Foiled Again

Layer the vegetables, seasonings, and fish in the center of the aluminum foil.

Fold the foil over the food, and seal tightly.

Southwestern Sole

Prep: 8 minutes   Cook: 18 minutes

1 pound sole fillets (or flounder)
Vegetable cooking spray
1 cup no-salt-added salsa
1 tablespoon chopped fresh cilantro
1 clove garlic, minced
½ cup (2 ounces) shredded Monterey Jack cheese with peppers
Fresh cilantro sprigs (optional)
Lime wedges (optional)

1 Arrange fish in an 11- x 7- x 1½-inch baking dish coated with cooking spray. Combine salsa, chopped cilantro, and garlic; spoon mixture over fish.

2 Bake, uncovered, at 350° for 15 minutes or until fish flakes easily when tested with a fork. Sprinkle with cheese; bake 3 additional minutes or until cheese melts. Remove fish from baking dish, using a slotted spoon. If desired, garnish with cilantro sprigs and lime wedges.
Yield: 4 servings.

Per Serving: Calories 179 (30% from fat)   Fat 6.0g (Sat 3.0g)   Protein 25.9g   Carbohydrate 4.4g   Fiber 0.0g   Cholesterol 65mg   Sodium 314mg

■ Turn down the heat by using regular Monterey Jack cheese instead of the kind with peppers.

Italian Red Snapper

Prep: 11 minutes   Cook: 25 minutes

4 (4-ounce) red snapper fillets
¼ cup dry white wine
¼ cup lemon juice
½ teaspoon dried oregano
½ teaspoon dried basil
¼ teaspoon salt
¼ teaspoon pepper
4 cloves garlic, minced
1 (14½-ounce) can no-salt-added diced tomatoes, drained

1 Place fish in an 11- x 7- x 1½-inch baking dish. Combine wine and next 6 ingredients, stirring well. Pour wine mixture and tomato over fish. Bake, uncovered, at 350° for 25 minutes or until fish flakes easily when tested with a fork.
Yield: 4 servings.

Per Serving: Calories 136 (11% from fat)   Fat 1.6g (Sat 0.3g)   Protein 24.1g   Carbohydrate 5.7g   Fiber 0.6g   Cholesterol 42mg   Sodium 229mg

■ This dish is truly a quick weeknight favorite because everything's already in your kitchen except the fish.

When you need a great dish to serve company, these salmon steaks are the answer. They're quick to prepare, look impressive on the table, and have a tangy-sweet flavor that your guests will rave about.

Glazed Salmon Steaks

Prep: 10 minutes   Marinate: 1 hour   Cook: 8 minutes

½ cup low-sodium soy sauce
⅓ cup dry sherry
1 clove garlic, crushed
8 (4-ounce) salmon steaks (½ inch thick)
⅓ cup firmly packed brown sugar
2 tablespoons honey
2 teaspoons vegetable oil
Vegetable cooking spray
Flowering chives (optional)

1 Combine first 3 ingredients in a large heavy-duty, zip-top plastic bag. Add fish; seal bag, and shake until fish is well coated. Marinate in refrigerator 1 hour, turning occasionally.

2 Remove fish from marinade, reserving 3 tablespoons marinade. Discard remaining marinade. Combine reserved marinade, brown sugar, honey, and oil in a small saucepan. Cook over medium heat until mixture comes to a boil and sugar dissolves.

3 Coat grill rack with cooking spray; place on grill over medium-hot coals (350° to 400°). Place fish on rack. Grill, covered, 4 to 5 minutes on each side or until fish flakes easily when tested with a fork, basting occasionally with brown sugar mixture. Garnish with flowering chives, if desired.
Yield: 8 servings.

Per Serving: Calories 248 (38% from fat)   Fat 10.6g (Sat 1.8g)   Protein 23.3g   Carbohydrate 13.3g   Fiber 0.0g   Cholesterol 74mg   Sodium 158mg

Parmesan-Romano Tilapia

Prep: 6 minutes   Cook: 10 minutes

¼ cup reduced-fat mayonnaise
1 tablespoon dried onion flakes
2 teaspoons low-sodium Worcestershire sauce
1 teaspoon Dijon mustard
1 teaspoon dry sherry
4 (4-ounce) tilapia fillets (or flounder or orange roughy)
Vegetable cooking spray
2 tablespoons grated Parmesan-Romano cheese blend

1 Combine first 5 ingredients, stirring well. Place fish in an
11- x 7- x 1½-inch baking dish coated with cooking spray. Spread
mayonnaise mixture over fish; sprinkle evenly with cheese. Bake,
uncovered, at 425° for 10 to 12 minutes or until fish flakes easily
when tested with a fork.
Yield: 4 servings.

Per Serving: Calories 172 (40% from fat)   Fat 7.6g (Sat 1.6g)   Protein 22.3g
Carbohydrate 2.8g   Fiber 0.1g   Cholesterol 87mg   Sodium 266mg

■ Tilapia, a popular fish in
Africa for many years, is now
raised all over the world. It's a
white-fleshed fish suitable for
baking, broiling, and grilling.
Tilapia is also called St. Peter's
fish and Hawaiian sunfish.

Soy-Lime Grilled Tuna

Prep: 10 minutes   Marinate: 30 minutes   Cook: 10 minutes

4 (4-ounce) tuna steaks (1 inch thick)
½ cup lime juice
¼ cup low-sodium soy sauce
1 teaspoon peeled, minced gingerroot
½ teaspoon dried crushed red pepper
Vegetable cooking spray

1 Place fish in a shallow baking dish. Combine lime juice and next
3 ingredients, stirring well. Pour lime juice mixture over fish. Cover
and marinate in refrigerator 30 minutes, turning fish once.

2 Remove fish from marinade; reserve marinade. Place marinade in
a small saucepan; bring to a boil, and set aside.

3 Coat grill rack with cooking spray; place on grill over medium-
hot coals (350° to 400°). Place fish on rack; grill, covered, 4 to 5
minutes on each side or until fish flakes easily when tested with a
fork, basting often with reserved marinade.
Yield: 4 servings.

Per Serving: Calories 162 (31% from fat)   Fat 5.5g (Sat 1.4g)   Protein 25.5g
Carbohydrate 0.7g   Fiber 0.0g   Cholesterol 42mg   Sodium 140mg

■ Let lime juice and soy sauce
be your tuna helpers. After only
30 minutes of marinating in
this tangy mixture, tuna goes
from "OK" to "Oh, Wow!"

■ Make the dipping sauce ahead, and store it in the refrigerator for up to three days.

Heads or Tails?

Split the lobster tail shell lengthwise using kitchen shears. Cut through the upper shell and lower shell.

Pull out the meat through the split shell.

Lobster Tails with Curried Chutney Dipping Sauce

Prep: 15 minutes   Cook: 12 minutes

4 (8-ounce) fresh or frozen lobster tails, thawed
1 pound fresh asparagus spears
½ cup unsweetened orange juice
1 teaspoon curry powder, divided
Vegetable cooking spray
¾ cup nonfat sour cream
¼ cup mango chutney
1 tablespoon chopped fresh cilantro

1 Split lobster shells lengthwise, cutting through hard upper shells and underneath shells with kitchen shears. Remove lobster meat through split shells. Discard shells.

2 Snap off tough ends of asparagus. Remove scales from stalks with a knife or vegetable peeler, if desired.

3 Combine juice and ½ teaspoon curry powder. Place asparagus and lobster tails on rack of a broiler pan coated with cooking spray. Brush one half of juice mixture over lobster and asparagus. Broil 5½ inches from heat (with electric oven door partially opened) 12 minutes, basting often with remaining juice mixture. Remove from oven; cut lobster meat into ½-inch-thick slices.

4 Combine remaining ½ teaspoon curry powder, sour cream, chutney, and cilantro, stirring well. Arrange asparagus spears and lobster slices on individual serving plates. Serve with chutney sauce.
Yield: 4 servings.

Per Serving: Calories 221 (4% from fat)   Fat 1.0g (Sat 0.2g)   Protein 25.2g
Carbohydrate 25.1g   Fiber 1.7g   Cholesterol 71mg   Sodium 580mg

Scallops over Parmesan Creamed Spinach

Prep: 22 minutes   Cook: 15 minutes

Vegetable cooking spray
1 cup sliced fresh mushrooms
1 (10-ounce) package frozen chopped spinach, thawed
¼ cup plus 2 tablespoons light process cream cheese
3 tablespoons skim milk
2 tablespoons reduced-fat Pesto-Parmesan salad dressing (such as
      Maple Grove Farms Lite Pesto-Parmesan dressing)
¼ teaspoon pepper
1 pound sea scallops
1½ tablespoons grated Parmesan cheese

1 Coat a nonstick skillet with cooking spray; place over medium-high heat until hot. Add mushrooms, and sauté until tender. Remove from heat, and set aside.

2 Drain spinach, and press between paper towels to remove excess moisture. Set aside.

3 Combine cream cheese and next 3 ingredients in a bowl; beat at medium speed of an electric mixer until creamy. Stir in mushrooms and spinach. Spoon spinach mixture into 4 individual gratin dishes coated with cooking spray; set aside.

4 Coat skillet with cooking spray; place over medium-high heat until hot. Add scallops, and cook 3 minutes, turning scallops to lightly brown on all sides. Place scallops evenly over spinach mixture in gratin dishes; sprinkle with Parmesan cheese. Bake at 375° for 15 minutes or until thoroughly heated and lightly browned.
Yield: 4 servings.

Per Serving: Calories 203 (31% from fat)   Fat 7.0g (Sat 2.9g)   Protein 25.0g
Carbohydrate 9.9g   Fiber 2.6g   Cholesterol 51mg   Sodium 475mg

No gratin dishes? No problem. Bake the spinach and scallop mixture in an 8-inch square baking dish.

Instead of soaking crusty French bread in the rich tomato sauce, spoon the mussels and sauce over steaming spaghetti (¾ cup per serving). The calories and fat will be about the same.

Mussels in Tomato Sauce

Prep: 10 minutes   Cook: 30 minutes

2 pounds fresh mussels
Olive-oil flavored vegetable cooking spray
2 teaspoons olive oil
3 tablespoons minced garlic
2 (14½-ounce) cans no-salt-added diced tomatoes, undrained
1 cup water
½ cup dry red wine
2 tablespoons chopped fresh parsley
½ teaspoon salt
½ teaspoon dried crushed red pepper
Fresh parsley sprigs (optional)
8 (1½-ounce) pieces French bread

1 Remove beards on mussels, and scrub shells with a brush. Discard opened, cracked, or heavy mussels (they're filled with sand). Set remaining mussels aside.

2 Coat a large nonstick skillet with cooking spray; add oil. Place over medium-high heat until hot. Add garlic; sauté 1 minute. Add tomato, water, and wine; bring to a boil. Reduce heat; simmer, uncovered, 20 minutes. Stir in chopped parsley, salt, and pepper. Add mussels. Cover and cook 5 minutes or until mussels open; discard unopened mussels. Garnish with parsley sprigs, if desired. Serve with French bread.
Yield: 8 servings.

Per Serving: Calories 223 (15% from fat)   Fat 3.8g (Sat 0.7g)   Protein 11.4g
Carbohydrate 35.3g   Fiber 1.2g   Cholesterol 15mg   Sodium 588mg

Mussels in Tomato Sauce

Spicy Shrimp Creole

Spicy Shrimp Creole

Prep: 20 minutes   Cook: 20 minutes

1 pound unpeeled medium-size fresh shrimp
Olive oil-flavored vegetable cooking spray
1 cup chopped onion
1 cup chopped green pepper
½ teaspoon dried crushed red pepper
6 cloves garlic, minced
2 (14½-ounce) cans Cajun-style stewed tomatoes, undrained
5 cups cooked long-grain rice (cooked without salt or fat)

1 Peel and devein shrimp; set aside.

2 Coat a nonstick skillet with cooking spray; place over medium-high heat until hot. Add onion and next 3 ingredients; sauté until tender. Add tomato. Bring to a boil; reduce heat, and simmer, uncovered, 10 minutes, stirring occasionally. Add shrimp. Cover and cook 5 minutes or until shrimp turn pink. Serve over rice.
Yield: 5 servings.

Per Serving: Calories 362 (4% from fat)   Fat 1.7g (Sat 0.3g)   Protein 20.0g
Carbohydrate 66.4g   Fiber 4.8g   Cholesterol 103mg   Sodium 748mg

■ Here are three ways to make this quick recipe even quicker:
1. Ask the grocer to peel and devein the shrimp.
2. Use frozen onion and green pepper instead of chopping fresh.
3. Prepare instant rice.

Quick Paella

Prep: 10 minutes   Cook: 23 minutes

1 dozen fresh mussels
2½ cups canned low-sodium chicken broth
1 cup converted rice, uncooked
1 tablespoon curry powder
¼ teaspoon salt
1 cup frozen English peas
2 (8-ounce) packages chunk-style lobster-flavored seafood product
1 (7½-ounce) jar whole pimientos, drained and cut into 1-inch
      pieces

1 Remove beards on mussels, and scrub shells with a brush. Discard opened, cracked, or heavy mussels (they're filled with sand). Set aside.

2 Place broth in a large saucepan, and bring to a boil; add rice, curry powder, and salt. Cover, reduce heat, and simmer 15 minutes. Add mussels, peas, seafood, and pimiento; cook 5 additional minutes or until mussels open and rice is tender. Discard unopened mussels.
Yield: 6 servings.

Per Serving: Calories 232 (6% from fat)   Fat 1.5g (Sat 0.4g)   Protein 13.2g
Carbohydrate 40.4g   Fiber 1.7g   Cholesterol 8mg   Sodium 697mg

■ Paella (a traditional Spanish dish) may have different combinations of seafood, meat, and vegetables tossed in, but it always has flavored rice. Use the converted (parboiled) kind in this recipe so your rice won't be gummy.

Grains
■ ■ ■
Pastas

Thank goodness these are modern times so I don't have to do all that harvesting, milling, grinding, rolling, and cutting just to get some rice or noodles.

I simply empty the contents of a box or a plastic bag into boiling water, and in 10 minutes I have tender pasta. And when I toss the pasta with a little cheese and a few cooked vegetables, I've got dinner. So much for the dark ages.

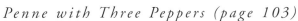

Penne with Three Peppers (page 103)

Portobello mushrooms are large, dark brown mushrooms. When they're cooked, they have a rich "meaty" flavor and texture.

■ Bulgur is similar to cracked wheat. Both are made from wheat kernels, but they're processed differently. Look for bulgur in the grain section of your grocery store.

Portobello Mushroom Barley

Prep: 17 minutes   Cook: 21 minutes

1 small leek (about ¼ pound)
Olive oil-flavored vegetable cooking spray
1 teaspoon olive oil
5 ounces fresh portobello mushrooms, chopped
1 clove garlic, minced
1 cup quick-cooking barley, uncooked
1⅔ cups canned no-salt-added beef broth
⅓ cup dry white wine
⅛ teaspoon salt
2 tablespoons grated Parmesan cheese

1 Remove and discard root, tough outer leaves, and top from leek. Finely chop leek.

2 Coat a large nonstick skillet with cooking spray; add oil. Place over medium heat until hot. Add chopped leek, mushrooms, and garlic; sauté until mushrooms are tender. Add barley and next 3 ingredients; bring to a boil. Cover, reduce heat, and simmer 16 to 18 minutes or until barley is tender and most of liquid is absorbed. Remove from heat; let stand 5 minutes. Sprinkle with cheese, and serve immediately.
Yield: 5 (¾-cup) servings.

Per Serving: Calories 118 (15% from fat)   Fat 2.0g (Sat 0.6g)   Protein 4.0g
Carbohydrate 20.9g   Fiber 4.0g   Cholesterol 2mg   Sodium 102mg

Bulgur Pilaf

Prep: 5 minutes   Cook: 20 minutes

2 cups canned no-salt-added chicken broth
1 cup bulgur, uncooked
¼ cup sliced green onions
2 tablespoons raisins
½ teaspoon salt
2 tablespoons sliced almonds, toasted

1 Place broth in a medium saucepan; bring to a boil. Add bulgur. Cover, reduce heat, and simmer 15 minutes. Stir in green onions, raisins, and salt; cover and cook 5 additional minutes or until bulgur is tender and liquid is absorbed. Stir in almonds.
Yield: 4 (¾-cup) servings.

Per Serving: Calories 200 (11% from fat)   Fat 2.5g (Sat 0.3g)   Protein 6.5g
Carbohydrate 39.8g   Fiber 8.6g   Cholesterol 0mg   Sodium 304mg

Mushroom Couscous

Prep: 5 minutes   Cook: 10 minutes

Butter-flavored vegetable cooking spray
4 cups sliced fresh mushrooms (about ¾ pound)
½ cup chopped onion
2 cloves garlic, minced
1 cup water
¼ teaspoon salt
⅛ teaspoon ground red pepper
⅔ cup couscous, uncooked

1 Coat a large saucepan with cooking spray; place over medium-high heat until hot. Add mushrooms, onion, and garlic; sauté until tender. Stir in water, salt, and pepper; bring to a boil. Remove saucepan from heat.

2 Stir in couscous; cover and let stand 5 minutes or until couscous is tender and liquid is absorbed. Fluff couscous with a fork.
Yield: 4 (1-cup) servings.

Per Serving: Calories 143 (5% from fat)   Fat 0.8g (Sat 0.1g)   Protein 6.1g   Carbohydrate 29.5g   Fiber 2.6g   Cholesterol 0mg   Sodium 153mg

If you haven't discovered couscous, you're missing out. It's a wheat grain that fluffs up like rice when it's cooked. The best part is that it takes only five minutes to cook.

Veggie Couscous

Prep: 10 minutes   Cook: 10 minutes

Vegetable cooking spray
½ cup diced carrot
½ cup chopped onion
1 (9-ounce) package frozen cut green beans, thawed
1 cup canned vegetable broth
½ cup water
¼ teaspoon salt
1 cup couscous, uncooked
2 tablespoons fat-free Italian dressing

1 Coat a nonstick skillet with cooking spray; place over medium-high heat until hot. Add carrot, onion, and beans. Sauté until tender.

2 Combine broth, water, and salt in a small saucepan; bring to a boil. Remove from heat. Add couscous; cover and let stand 5 minutes or until couscous is tender and liquid is absorbed. Fluff couscous with a fork. Add vegetable mixture and Italian dressing; toss lightly.
Yield: 6 (1-cup) servings.

Per Serving: Calories 134 (5% from fat)   Fat 0.7g (Sat 0.0g)   Protein 4.7g   Carbohydrate 28.3g   Fiber 3.3g   Cholesterol 0mg   Sodium 335mg

Southerners will say, "This tastes just like cheese grits!" Everyone else will say, "Can we have some more?"

Cheesy Farina
Prep: 13 minutes   Cook: 20 minutes

3 cups skim milk
¾ cup instant farina (such as Cream of Wheat), uncooked
1 cup freshly grated Parmesan cheese, divided
1¼ teaspoons dry mustard
½ cup egg substitute
¼ teaspoon salt
Vegetable cooking spray

1 Place milk in a medium saucepan; bring to a simmer. (Do not boil.) Gradually add farina, stirring constantly. Bring to a boil; reduce heat, and simmer, stirring constantly, 2 minutes or until thickened. Add ¾ cup cheese and mustard, stirring until cheese melts. Add egg substitute and salt; stir well with a wire whisk.

2 Spread farina mixture in an 8-inch square baking dish coated with cooking spray. Sprinkle remaining ¼ cup cheese over farina mixture. Bake at 400° for 20 to 25 minutes or until set.
Yield: 8 (½-cup) servings.

Per Serving: Calories 176 (20% from fat)   Fat 4.0g (Sat 2.4g)   Protein 12.1g
Carbohydrate 21.9g   Fiber 0.7g   Cholesterol 11mg   Sodium 441mg

■ ■ ■

Pan-Fried Farina: Prepare recipe as directed. Cover and chill. Remove farina from dish, and cut into 8 squares. Coat a nonstick skillet with cooking spray. Place over medium heat until hot. Add 4 farina squares. Cook 3 to 4 minutes on each side or until browned. Repeat procedure with remaining farina squares. Serve farina with no-salt-added salsa, if desired.

Ham and Grits Casserole

Prep: 15 minutes   Cook: 50 minutes

■ This cheesy side dish is also great as a main dish. You'll get four entrée servings with about 333 calories and 10.6 grams of fat per serving.

4 cups water
¼ teaspoon salt
1 cup quick-cooking grits, uncooked
1 cup chopped reduced-fat, low-salt ham
3 tablespoons reduced-calorie margarine
1 teaspoon low-sodium Worcestershire sauce
1 cup egg substitute
Vegetable cooking spray
½ cup (2 ounces) shredded reduced-fat sharp Cheddar cheese

1 Combine 4 cups water and salt in a large saucepan; bring to a boil. Stir in grits; cover, reduce heat, and simmer 5 minutes or until grits are thickened, stirring occasionally. Remove from heat. Add ham, margarine, and Worcestershire sauce; stir until margarine melts. Gradually add egg substitute, stirring well.

2 Spoon grits mixture into an 11- x 7- x 1½-inch baking dish coated with cooking spray. Bake at 350° for 45 minutes. Sprinkle with cheese. Bake 5 additional minutes or until cheese melts. Let stand 5 minutes before serving.
Yield: 8 (¾-cup) servings.

Per Serving: Calories 166 (29% from fat)   Fat 5.3g (Sat 1.8g)   Protein 10.6g
Carbohydrate 19.5g   Fiber 1.1g   Cholesterol 14mg   Sodium 365mg

Ham and Grits Casserole

Serve this jambalaya-like side dish with chicken or pork.

Quick Red Rice

Prep: 5 minutes   Cook: 15 minutes

Vegetable cooking spray
2 teaspoons vegetable oil
1¼ cups chopped onion
¾ cup chopped Canadian bacon
1 (10¾-ounce) can reduced-sodium, reduced-fat tomato soup
1½ cups water
1 cup instant rice, uncooked
¼ teaspoon pepper
¼ teaspoon hot sauce
⅛ teaspoon salt

1 Coat a medium saucepan with cooking spray; add oil. Place over medium-high heat until hot. Add onion and Canadian bacon; sauté 5 minutes or until onion is tender.

2 Stir in soup and water. Bring to a boil. Add rice and remaining ingredients. Cover, reduce heat, and simmer 10 minutes or until rice is tender and liquid is absorbed.
Yield: 4 (1-cup) servings.

Per Serving: Calories 212 (23% from fat)   Fat 5.4g (Sat 1.3g)   Protein 8.6g
Carbohydrate 32.8g   Fiber 1.6g   Cholesterol 13mg   Sodium 667mg

When you cook rice in orange juice and broth, you add flavor without fat.

Orange Rice Pilaf

Prep: 10 minutes   Cook: 20 minutes

1 teaspoon olive oil
¼ cup chopped onion
1 cup long-grain rice, uncooked
1 cup canned no-salt-added chicken broth
1 cup unsweetened orange juice
½ cup golden raisins
1 tablespoon grated orange rind
¼ teaspoon salt
¼ teaspoon freshly ground pepper

1 Heat oil in a medium nonstick skillet. Add onion; sauté until tender. Add rice to skillet; stir well. Cook, stirring constantly, 2 minutes. Add broth, juice, and raisins. Bring to a boil; cover, reduce heat, and simmer 20 to 25 minutes or until rice is tender and liquid is absorbed. Add orange rind, salt, and pepper; toss lightly.
Yield: 5 (¾-cup) servings.

Per Serving: Calories 223 (5% from fat)   Fat 1.3g (Sat 0.2g)   Protein 3.8g
Carbohydrate 49.8g   Fiber 1.5g   Cholesterol 0mg   Sodium 123mg

Mexican Rice Casserole

Prep: 10 minutes   Cook: 55 minutes

2 cups water
1 cup long-grain rice, uncooked
¼ cup skim milk
⅛ teaspoon salt
1 (10¾-ounce) can reduced-sodium, reduced-fat cream of
    mushroom soup
1 (4½-ounce) can chopped green chiles, drained
1½ cups (6 ounces) shredded reduced-fat Monterey Jack cheese
Vegetable cooking spray
⅛ teaspoon paprika

1 Place water in a saucepan· bring to a boil. Stir in rice. Cover, reduce heat, and simmer 20 ninutes or until rice is tender and liquid is absorbed. Add milk and next 3 ingredients; stir. Stir in 1 cup cheese.

2 Spoon mixture into an 11- x 7- x 1½-inch baking dish coated with cooking spray. Cover and bake at 350° for 30 minutes. Uncover; sprinkle with remaining cheese and paprika. Bake 5 additional minutes. **Yield: 8 (½-cup) servings.**

Per Serving: Calories 175 (27% from fat)   Fat 5.2g (Sat 2.7g)   Protein 8.9g Carbohydrate 22.8g   Fiber 0.7g   Cholesterol 17mg   Sodium 374mg

■ For variety, use reduced-fat sharp Cheddar cheese instead of Monterey Jack.

Texas Beans and Rice

Prep: 15 minutes   Cook: 12 minutes

1 cup instant brown rice, uncooked
Vegetable cooking spray
1 teaspoon vegetable oil
1 cup chopped onion
1 cup chopped green pepper
2 (16-ounce) cans chili hot beans, undrained
¾ cup fat-free barbecue sauce
¼ cup brewed coffee

1 Cook rice according to package directions, omitting salt and fat.

2 Coat a large nonstick skillet with cooking spray; add oil. Place over medium-high heat until hot. Add onion and pepper; sauté until tender. Add rice, beans, barbecue sauce, and coffee. Bring to a boil; reduce heat, and simmer, uncovered, 5 minutes or until thoroughly heated. **Yield: 8 (¾-cup) servings.**

Per Serving: Calories 125 (10% from fat)   Fat 1.4g (Sat 0.4g)   Protein 3.7g Carbohydrate 24.3g   Fiber 3.7g   Cholesterol 0mg   Sodium 595mg

■ Package directions on different brands of instant brown rice may vary slightly, but the cooking time is usually about 10 minutes.

Wild Rice-Vegetable Medley

Wild Rice-Vegetable Medley

Prep: 10 minutes   Cook: 15 minutes

Olive oil-flavored vegetable cooking spray
2 teaspoons olive oil
1 cup chopped green pepper
¾ cup chopped onion
¾ cup finely chopped carrot
1 (8-ounce) package sliced fresh mushrooms
1 (2¾-ounce) package instant wild rice, uncooked
1⅓ cups canned no-salt-added chicken broth
¼ teaspoon salt
¼ teaspoon pepper
Fresh flat-leaf parsley leaves (optional)

1 Coat a saucepan with cooking spray; add oil. Place over medium-high heat until hot. Add green pepper and next 3 ingredients; sauté until carrot is tender. Add rice and broth. Bring to a boil; reduce heat. Simmer, uncovered, 5 minutes or until liquid is absorbed. Stir in salt and pepper. Let stand 5 minutes. Garnish with parsley, if desired.
Yield: 5 (¾-cup) servings.

Per Serving: Calories 157 (15% from fat)   Fat 2.6g (Sat 0.3g)   Protein 4.1g
Carbohydrate 22.4g   Fiber 3.1g   Cholesterol 0mg   Sodium 128mg

■ For a quick and easy entrée, stir in 1 cup chopped cooked chicken.

Pesto Gemelli

Prep: 4 minutes   Cook: 14 minutes

2 tablespoons all-purpose flour
¾ cup evaporated skimmed milk, divided
¼ cup dry white wine
2 tablespoons pesto
¼ teaspoon salt
¼ teaspoon cracked pepper
6 ounces gemelli (small pasta twists), uncooked
1½ tablespoons freshly grated Parmesan cheese

1 Combine flour and ¼ cup milk in a small saucepan, stirring until smooth. Gradually add remaining milk and wine. Cook over medium heat, stirring constantly, until thickened and bubbly. Add pesto, salt, and pepper, stirring well.

2 Cook pasta according to package directions, omitting salt and fat; drain. Add pesto mixture; toss well. Sprinkle with cheese.
Yield: 4 (¾-cup) servings.

Per Serving: Calories 261 (18% from fat)   Fat 5.3g (Sat 1.3g)   Protein 11.3g
Carbohydrate 42.0g   Fiber 1.5g   Cholesterol 4mg   Sodium 326mg

■ You could make your own pesto with basil, Parmesan cheese, olive oil, and pine nuts. But the kind you can buy in a plastic container from the grocery store makes prep time quicker. Look for it near the refrigerated fresh pasta.

Garlic and Onion Roasting Guide

You can roast the garlic and onion a couple of days ahead, and store in the refrigerator.

Peel the papery outer skin from the head of garlic. Cut off the top fourth of the head.

Place the peeled garlic and onion in the center of the foil, and coat with cooking spray. Seal foil, and bake for 1 hour. Remove the skin from garlic.

Scoop out the soft garlic pulp.

Roasted Garlic and Onion Linguine

Prep: 11 minutes Cook: 1 hour

2 small onions (about ½ pound)
1 small head garlic
Olive oil-flavored vegetable cooking spray
¼ cup grated Parmesan cheese
¼ cup canned no-salt-added chicken broth
2 teaspoons olive oil
½ teaspoon cracked pepper
¼ teaspoon salt
12 ounces linguine, uncooked

1 Peel onions, and cut each into 8 wedges. Gently peel outer skin from garlic and discard. Cut off and discard top one-fourth of garlic head. Place onion and garlic, cut sides up, in center of a piece of heavy-duty aluminum foil; coat with cooking spray. Fold foil over onion and garlic, sealing tightly. Bake at 350° for 1 hour or until onion and garlic are soft. Remove from oven, and let cool.

2 Remove and discard skin from garlic. Scoop out garlic pulp with a small spoon. Position knife blade in food processor bowl; add garlic pulp, onion, and cheese. Pulse 5 times or until combined. Add broth and next 3 ingredients to garlic mixture. Process until mixture is finely chopped. Set aside.

3 Cook pasta according to package directions, omitting salt and fat; drain. Add garlic mixture; toss lightly. Serve immediately.
Yield: 8 (¾-cup) servings. *(Pasta pictured on page 22.)*

Per Serving: Calories 198 (12% from fat) Fat 2.7g (Sat 0.7g) Protein 7.1g
Carbohydrate 35.9g Fiber 1.6g Cholesterol 2mg Sodium 125mg

Creamy Macaroni and Cheese

Prep: 23 minutes   Cook: 15 minutes

1 (8-ounce) package elbow macaroni, uncooked
2 tablespoons reduced-calorie margarine
2 cups frozen chopped onion, celery, and pepper blend, thawed
2½ cups 1% low-fat milk
¼ cup all-purpose flour
1¼ cups (5 ounces) shredded reduced-fat sharp Cheddar cheese,
      divided
½ teaspoon salt
¼ teaspoon pepper
Vegetable cooking spray

1 Cook macaroni according to package directions, omitting salt and fat; drain, set aside, and keep warm.

2 Melt margarine in a large saucepan over medium-high heat. Add vegetables; sauté until tender. Reduce heat to medium. Combine milk and flour, stirring until smooth. Add milk mixture to vegetable mixture. Cook, stirring constantly, 10 to 15 minutes or until thickened and bubbly. Remove from heat. Add 1 cup cheese, salt, and pepper, stirring until cheese melts. Add macaroni to cheese mixture; stir well.

3 Spoon macaroni mixture into a 1½-quart baking dish coated with cooking spray. Sprinkle with remaining ¼ cup cheese. Cover and bake at 375° for 15 to 20 minutes or until bubbly. Let stand 10 minutes before serving.
Yield: 8 (¾-cup) servings.

Per Serving: Calories 231 (26% from fat)   Fat 6.6g (Sat 2.8g)   Protein 12.2g
Carbohydrate 30.6g   Fiber 0.8g   Cholesterol 15mg   Sodium 352mg

■ For a hearty one-dish meal, stir in 2 cups cubed reduced-fat, low-salt ham.

■ Save time by purchasing broccoli flowerets in the produce section or chopped broccoli and red pepper from the salad bar.

Hot Sesame Spaghetti
Prep: 10 minutes   Cook: 10 minutes

Vegetable cooking spray
2 teaspoons hot chile oil, divided
2½ cups coarsely chopped broccoli flowerets
1 cup diced sweet red pepper
½ cup chopped green onions
1½ teaspoons minced garlic
8 ounces spaghetti, uncooked
1 tablespoon sesame seeds, lightly toasted
½ teaspoon salt

1 Coat a large nonstick skillet with cooking spray; add 1 teaspoon oil. Place over medium-high heat until hot. Add broccoli and next 3 ingredients; sauté until vegetables are crisp-tender.

2 Cook pasta according to package directions, omitting salt and fat; drain well. Toss with remaining 1 teaspoon oil. Add broccoli mixture, sesame seeds, and salt; toss well.
Yield: 6 (1-cup) servings.

Per Serving: Calories 181 (15% from fat)   Fat 3.1g (Sat 0.5g)   Protein 6.5g   Carbohydrate 32.2g   Fiber 2.5g   Cholesterol 0mg   Sodium 209mg

Hot Sesame Spaghetti

Penne with Three Peppers

Prep: 17 minutes   Cook: 5 minutes

10 ounces penne (short tubular pasta), uncooked
Vegetable cooking spray
1 large sweet red pepper, seeded and cut into 4 pieces
1 large sweet yellow pepper, seeded and cut into 4 pieces
1 large green pepper, seeded and cut into 4 pieces
⅓ cup fat-free balsamic vinaigrette
1 (15-ounce) can cannellini beans, drained
½ cup crumbled feta cheese
Fresh basil sprigs (optional)

1 Cook pasta according to package directions, omitting salt and fat; drain. Place pasta in a large serving bowl. Set aside, and keep warm.

2 Place pepper pieces on a baking sheet coated with cooking spray. Broil 3 inches from heat (with electric oven door partially opened) 5 to 6 minutes or until tender, turning once. Cut peppers into 1-inch pieces.

3 Add peppers, vinaigrette, beans, and cheese to pasta; toss well. Garnish with fresh basil, if desired.
Yield: 8 (1-cup) servings. *(Recipe pictured on page 90.)*

Grilling Instructions: Arrange peppers in a grilling basket coated with cooking spray. Place grill rack on grill over medium-hot coals (350° to 400°). Place grilling basket on rack; grill, covered, 10 to 12 minutes or until vegetables are tender, turning once. Proceed with recipe as directed.

Per Serving: Calories 211 (11% from fat)   Fat 2.6g (Sat 1.2g)   Protein 7.8g
Carbohydrate 38.3g   Fiber 3.2g   Cholesterol 6mg   Sodium 329mg

■ If you don't have fat-free balsamic vinaigrette, use another fat-free vinaigrette or fat-free Italian dressing.

> Need a quick kid-pleasing meal? This creamy spaghetti baked as a pie will satisfy even your pickiest eater's appetite.

Spaghetti-Ham Pie

Prep: 18 minutes   Cook: 15 minutes

6 ounces spaghetti, uncooked
Vegetable cooking spray
¾ cup chopped reduced-fat, low-salt ham
¾ cup sliced fresh mushrooms
½ teaspoon minced garlic
2 tablespoons all-purpose flour
¼ teaspoon salt
⅛ teaspoon pepper
1 (12-ounce) can evaporated skimmed milk
1 cup (4 ounces) finely shredded reduced-fat Swiss cheese, divided

1 Cook pasta according to package directions, omitting salt and fat; drain and set aside.

2 Coat a nonstick skillet with cooking spray; place over medium-high heat until hot. Add ham, mushrooms, and garlic; sauté until mushrooms are tender. Stir in flour, salt, and pepper. Cook, stirring constantly, 1 minute. Add milk, and cook over medium heat, stirring constantly, until thickened. Combine ham mixture, pasta, and ½ cup cheese. Spoon into a 9-inch pieplate coated with cooking spray; sprinkle with remaining cheese. Bake, uncovered, at 425° for 15 minutes. Let stand 5 minutes. Slice into wedges.
Yield: 6 servings.

Per Serving: Calories 245 (19% from fat)   Fat 5.1g (Sat 2.3g)   Protein 18.3g
Carbohydrate 31.1g   Fiber 0.9g   Cholesterol 23mg   Sodium 341mg

Spaghetti-Ham Pie

Asian Noodles

Prep: 8 minutes Cook: 4 minutes Chill: 2 hours

3 quarts water
1 (7-ounce) package rice vermicelli, uncooked
3 tablespoons low-sodium soy sauce
2 tablespoons honey
2 teaspoons dark sesame oil, divided
Vegetable cooking spray
1 cup diagonally sliced green onions
1 tablespoon peeled, minced gingerroot
1 teaspoon toasted sesame seeds

1 Bring 3 quarts water to a boil in a large saucepan; add pasta, and cook 3 minutes or until tender. Drain. Place pasta in a serving bowl.

2 Combine soy sauce, honey, and 1 teaspoon oil; stir well with a wire whisk. Add soy sauce mixture to pasta; toss well.

3 Coat a large nonstick skillet with cooking spray; add remaining 1 teaspoon oil. Place over medium-high heat until hot. Add green onions and gingerroot; sauté 1 minute or until tender. Add onion mixture to pasta mixture; toss lightly. Serve warm or chilled. Sprinkle with sesame seeds just before serving.
Yield: 8 (¾-cup) servings.

Per Serving: Calories 224 (13% from fat) Fat 3.2g (Sat 0.7g) Protein 4.5g
Carbohydrate 44.3g Fiber 0.2g Cholesterol 0mg Sodium 149mg

Rice vermicelli is a type of noodle made from rice flour. It's also called long rice, Chinese vermicelli, and rice sticks.

Meatless Main Dishes

I used to think of a meatless dish as something made from ingredients found only in health food stores. Not anymore. Meatless simply means that I can use vegetables, grains, pasta, eggs, and cheese in all kinds of tasty, filling combinations.

For quick meatless meals, I keep vegetables in the freezer, cheese in the refrigerator, and canned beans in the pantry. Think about all the time you'll save not fretting over which cuts of meat have the least fat.

Black Bean Lasagna Roll (page 117)

107

If you don't have individual gratin dishes, cook this cheesy vegetable casserole in a shallow 1-quart baking dish instead.

Curried Vegetable Gratin

Prep: 15 minutes   Cook: 4 minutes

1 (16-ounce) package frozen carrots, cauliflower, and
      snow pea pods (or other frozen vegetable combination)
2 tablespoons all-purpose flour
1⅓ cups skim milk, divided
1 tablespoon reduced-calorie margarine
½ cup (2 ounces) shredded reduced-fat Swiss cheese
½ teaspoon curry powder
¼ teaspoon salt
Vegetable cooking spray
2 tablespoons fine, dry breadcrumbs

1 Arrange frozen vegetables in a steamer basket over boiling water. Cover and steam 8 minutes or until crisp-tender; drain. Set aside, and keep warm.

2 Combine flour and ⅓ cup milk in a saucepan, stirring until smooth. Add remaining 1 cup milk and margarine; stir well. Cook over medium heat, stirring constantly, until milk mixture is thickened and bubbly. Remove from heat; add Swiss cheese, curry powder, and salt, stirring until cheese melts.

3 Spoon vegetables evenly into 4 (1½-cup) gratin or baking dishes coated with cooking spray. Spoon cheese mixture over vegetables. Sprinkle with breadcrumbs. Broil 5½ inches from heat (with electric oven door partially opened) 4 to 5 minutes or until lightly browned. **Yield: 4 servings.**

Per Serving: Calories 153 (28% from fat)   Fat 4.8g (Sat 1.8g)   Protein 10.9g Carbohydrate 17.3g   Fiber 2.8g   Cholesterol 10mg   Sodium 299mg

Vegetarian Egg Rolls

Prep: 15 minutes   **Cook:** 10 minutes

Vegetable cooking spray
5 cups finely preshredded cabbage
1 (14-ounce) can Chinese vegetables, drained
7 ounces soft tofu
1 tablespoon hoisin sauce
8 egg roll wrappers
2 teaspoons sesame oil, divided
½ cup Chinese sweet-and-sour sauce

1 Coat a large nonstick skillet with cooking spray; place over medium heat until hot. Add cabbage and Chinese vegetables; sauté 5 minutes or until cabbage is tender. Combine vegetable mixture, tofu, and hoisin sauce, stirring well.

2 Spoon vegetable mixture evenly into centers of egg roll wrappers. For each egg roll, fold one corner of wrapper over filling; then fold left and right corners of wrapper over filling. Push filling toward center of wrapper. Lightly brush exposed corner of wrapper with water. Tightly roll filled end of wrapper toward exposed corner; lightly press corner to seal securely.

3 Coat skillet with cooking spray; add 1 teaspoon sesame oil. Place over medium heat until hot. Add 4 egg rolls; cook 4 to 5 minutes or until golden, turning occasionally. Repeat procedure with remaining 1 teaspoon oil and 4 egg rolls. Serve with sweet-and-sour sauce.
Yield: 4 servings (serving size: 2 egg rolls).

Per Serving: Calories 307 (11% from fat)   Fat 3.9g (Sat 0.6g)   Protein 10.1g   Carbohydrate 58.5g   Fiber 3.5g   Cholesterol 0mg   Sodium 540mg

How to Roll an Egg Roll

Rolling an egg roll is as easy as wrapping a package when you follow the simple steps below.

Spoon the vegetable mixture into the center of the wrapper, and fold one corner of the wrapper over the filling.

Fold the left and right corners of the wrapper over the filling, making an envelope. Brush the unfolded wrapper corner with water.

Roll the filled end toward the exposed corner, and press the corner to seal the package.

This crispy hash brown patty topped with cheese, nuts, and "meaty-tasting" mushrooms will satisfy both meat *and* potato lovers. (See the description and photograph of portobello mushrooms on page 92.)

Portobello-Potato Pancake

Prep: 10 minutes   Cook: 30 minutes

1 (26-ounce) bag frozen shredded hash brown potatoes, thawed
1 small onion, thinly sliced
½ teaspoon salt
½ teaspoon freshly ground pepper
Olive oil-flavored vegetable cooking spray
2 teaspoons olive oil, divided
6 ounces fresh portobello mushrooms, thinly sliced
1 (14-ounce) can artichoke hearts, drained and chopped
½ cup (2 ounces) freshly grated Asiago cheese, divided
2 tablespoons coarsely chopped walnuts
Fresh rosemary sprigs (optional)

1 Combine first 4 ingredients in a large bowl, stirring well. Coat a 12-inch nonstick skillet with cooking spray. Add 1 teaspoon oil; place over medium heat until hot. Spoon potato mixture into skillet; press to smooth top. Cook 8 minutes or until potato is crisp and browned on bottom. Invert potato pancake onto a baking sheet.

2 Coat skillet with cooking spray; add remaining 1 teaspoon oil. Place over medium heat until hot. Return pancake to skillet, uncooked side down. Cook 8 minutes or until crisp and browned. Invert pancake onto baking sheet coated with cooking spray; set aside, and keep warm.

3 Coat skillet with cooking spray; place over medium-high heat until hot. Add mushrooms, and sauté 2 minutes or until tender. Remove from heat, and stir in artichoke.

4 Sprinkle pancake with ¼ cup cheese. Top with mushroom mixture. Sprinkle with walnuts; top with remaining ¼ cup cheese. Bake at 350° for 12 minutes or until thoroughly heated. Cut into 8 wedges. Garnish with fresh rosemary sprigs, if desired.
Yield: 4 servings (serving size: 2 wedges).

Per Serving: Calories 296 (29% from fat)   Fat 9.5g (Sat 2.9g)   Protein 11.7g
Carbohydrate 43.7g   Fiber 2.8g   Cholesterol 10mg   Sodium 737mg

Portobello-Potato Pancake

Reduce the cook time by baking the potatoes in the microwave oven. For four potatoes, microwave at HIGH for 12 to 14 minutes.

Grecian Stuffed Potatoes

Prep: 15 minutes   Cook: 45 minutes

4 (8-ounce) baking potatoes
1 (15-ounce) can no-salt-added garbanzo beans, drained
¼ cup plus 2 tablespoons water
¼ cup plus 1 tablespoon fresh lemon juice, divided
1½ teaspoons no-salt-added Greek seasoning, divided
½ teaspoon salt, divided
3 cups diced tomato
3 tablespoons sliced ripe olives
¼ teaspoon pepper
½ cup crumbled reduced-fat feta cheese

1 Scrub potatoes; prick each several times with a fork. Bake at 400° for 45 minutes or until done.

2 Position knife blade in food processor bowl; add beans, water, ¼ cup lemon juice, ½ teaspoon Greek seasoning, and ¼ teaspoon salt. Process 1 minute or until smooth. Combine remaining 1 tablespoon lemon juice, 1 teaspoon seasoning, and ¼ teaspoon salt; add tomato, olives, and pepper, stirring well.

3 Cut a lengthwise slit in top of each potato. Press ends of each potato toward center, pushing pulp up. Top potatoes evenly with bean mixture and tomato mixture; sprinkle with cheese.
Yield: 4 servings.

Per Serving: Calories 364 (14% from fat)   Fat 5.9g (Sat 2.1g)   Protein 15.5g   Carbohydrate 66.3g   Fiber 8.1g   Cholesterol 6mg   Sodium 645mg

Grecian Stuffed Potatoes

Vegetable-Cheese Pie

Prep: 10 minutes   Cook: 45 minutes

4½ cups frozen shredded hash brown potatoes, thawed
1 cup (4 ounces) shredded reduced-fat Cheddar cheese
¼ cup finely chopped green pepper
¼ cup chopped tomato
3 tablespoons finely chopped onion
¾ cup skim milk
¾ cup egg substitute
½ teaspoon salt
¼ teaspoon pepper
Vegetable cooking spray

1 Combine first 9 ingredients in a large bowl, stirring well. Pour mixture into a 9-inch pieplate coated with cooking spray. Bake, uncovered, at 350° for 45 minutes or until a knife inserted in center comes out clean. Let stand 10 minutes.
Yield: 4 servings.

Per Serving: Calories 201 (26% from fat)   Fat 5.7g (Sat 3.2g)   Protein 15.9g   Carbohydrate 21.3g   Fiber 0.9g   Cholesterol 19mg   Sodium 603mg

■ Keep a bag of shredded potatoes and a carton of egg substitute in the freezer so that you can whip up this pie for a casual brunch or lunch. Vary the vegetables depending on what's in your refrigerator.

Roasted Vegetable Pot Pie

Prep: 30 minutes   Cook: 30 minutes

2 (16-ounce) packages frozen stew vegetables, thawed
2 tablespoons fat-free Italian dressing
1 (25¾-ounce) jar fat-free chunky spaghetti sauce with mushrooms and sweet peppers
1 (15-ounce) can dark red kidney beans, drained
1 (10-ounce) can refrigerated pizza crust dough
1 teaspoon fennel seeds

1 Combine vegetables and Italian dressing, tossing well. Spoon vegetable mixture onto a large baking sheet. Bake at 450° for 20 minutes or until vegetables are lightly browned, stirring once. Remove from oven. Reduce oven temperature to 375°. Combine roasted vegetable mixture, spaghetti sauce, and kidney beans, stirring well. Spoon vegetable mixture into a 13- x 9- x 2-inch baking dish.

2 Unroll dough onto a work surface; sprinkle dough with fennel seeds. Roll dough to a 14- x 10-inch rectangle; place over vegetable mixture. Bake at 375° for 30 minutes or until lightly browned.
Yield: 6 servings.

Per Serving: Calories 297 (6% from fat)   Fat 1.9g (Sat 0.4g)   Protein 12.0g   Carbohydrate 57.9g   Fiber 5.1g   Cholesterol 0mg   Sodium 875mg

■ Roasting the frozen stew vegetables intensifies their flavor and keeps them from becoming too soft when they're baked in the pie.

If you can't find roasted garlic-flavored oil, use regular vegetable oil and add ½ teaspoon minced garlic. The garlic flavor, along with tomatoes and olive oil, is a trademark of dishes from Provence—a region in the southeastern part of France.

Spaghetti Squash with White Bean Provençal

Prep: 20 minutes   Cook: 45 minutes

1 (2½-pound) spaghetti squash
Vegetable cooking spray
1 teaspoon roasted garlic-flavored vegetable oil
2 cups thinly sliced leek (about 1 leek)
2 (16-ounce) cans navy beans, drained
1 (14½-ounce) can no-salt-added stewed tomatoes, undrained
2 tablespoons chopped ripe olives
1 tablespoon balsamic vinegar
¼ teaspoon salt
¼ teaspoon pepper
Fresh celery leaves (optional)

1 Wash squash; cut in half lengthwise. Remove and discard seeds. Place squash, cut sides down, in a 13- x 9- x 2-inch baking dish coated with cooking spray. Bake at 350° for 45 minutes or until tender; let cool slightly. Using a fork, remove spaghetti-like strands from squash; discard shells. Place strands on a platter; set aside, and keep warm.

2 Coat a saucepan with cooking spray; add oil. Place over medium-high heat until hot. Add leek; sauté 3 minutes or until tender. Add beans and tomato; cook over medium heat 5 minutes. Stir in olives and next 3 ingredients; cook until thoroughly heated. Spoon bean mixture over squash. Garnish with fresh celery leaves, if desired.
Yield: 4 servings.

Per Serving: Calories 226 (11% from fat)   Fat 2.9g (Sat 0.6g)   Protein 10.5g
Carbohydrate 43.0g   Fiber 6.8g   Cholesterol 0mg   Sodium 508mg

Spaghetti Squash with White Bean Provençal

Working with Wontons

Using wonton wrappers to hold the filling for ravioli is a lot easier than making pasta.

Make a star design by placing 1 wonton wrapper on top of another.

Place the cheese mixture in the center of the wonton star.

Moisten the edges of the wrappers with water, and fold the wrappers in half, bringing the moistened edges together. Press firmly.

Italian Wonton Ravioli

Prep: 20 minutes   Cook: 15 minutes

Olive-oil flavored vegetable cooking spray
1 cup chopped green pepper
2 cloves garlic, minced
2 cups fat-free chunky spaghetti sauce with mushrooms
      and sweet peppers
½ cup water
½ cup nonfat ricotta cheese
½ cup crumbled basil- and tomato-flavored feta cheese
      (or regular feta)
1½ tablespoons pesto
24 wonton wrappers
2 quarts water

1 Coat a large nonstick skillet with cooking spray; place over medium-high heat until hot. Add chopped pepper and garlic; sauté 2 minutes. Add spaghetti sauce and ½ cup water. Bring to a boil; reduce heat, and simmer, uncovered, 10 minutes, stirring occasionally. Set aside, and keep warm.

2 Combine cheeses and pesto in a small bowl. Place 1 wonton wrapper on a work surface. Place a second wrapper (at a one-quarter turn) on top of first wrapper, creating a star design. Place 1 tablespoon cheese mixture in center of star. Moisten edges of wrappers with water; fold in half, bringing edges together. Press firmly. Repeat procedure with remaining wrappers and cheese mixture.

3 Bring 2 quarts water to a boil in a large saucepan over high heat. Add half of wontons; boil, uncovered, 1 minute. Remove from water, using a slotted spoon; set aside, and keep warm. Repeat procedure with remaining wontons. To serve, spoon one-fourth of spaghetti sauce mixture onto each plate. Top each serving with 3 wontons. Serve immediately.
Yield: 4 servings.

Per Serving: Calories 310 (25% from fat)   Fat 8.5g (Sat 3.9g)   Protein 15.5g Carbohydrate 43.8g   Fiber 1.8g   Cholesterol 27mg   Sodium 990mg

Black Bean Lasagna Rolls

Prep: 28 minutes   **Cook:** 25 minutes

1 cup (4 ounces) shredded reduced-fat Monterey Jack cheese
1 (15-ounce) carton part-skim ricotta cheese
1 (4½-ounce) can chopped green chiles, drained
½ teaspoon chili powder
⅛ teaspoon salt
8 lasagna noodles, uncooked
2 cups canned drained no-salt-added black beans
Vegetable cooking spray
1 (15½-ounce) jar no-salt-added salsa
Fresh cilantro sprigs (optional)

1 Combine first 5 ingredients, stirring well.

2 Cook lasagna noodles according to package directions, omitting salt and fat; drain well.

3 Spread cheese mixture over one side of each noodle. Spoon black beans evenly over cheese mixture. Roll up noodles, jellyroll fashion, beginning at narrow ends.

4 Place lasagna rolls, seam sides down, in an 11- x 7- x 1½-inch baking dish coated with cooking spray. Pour salsa over rolls. Cover and bake at 350° for 25 minutes or until thoroughly heated. Garnish with cilantro sprigs, if desired.
Yield: 8 servings.   *(Recipe pictured on cover.)*

Per Serving: Calories 295 (24% from fat)   Fat 7.8g (Sat 4.3g)   Protein 18.8g   Carbohydrate 37.8g   Fiber 2.8g   Cholesterol 26mg   Sodium 387mg

■ Serve these cheese- and bean-filled lasagna rolls with a mixed green salad for a hearty meatless meal.

The great thing about this lasagna is that you don't have to cook anything but the noodles before you layer the ingredients in the dish.

Spinach Lasagna

Prep: 20 minutes   Cook: 30 minutes

2 cups 1% low-fat cottage cheese
½ cup egg substitute
2 (10-ounce) packages frozen chopped spinach, thawed and drained well
1 (25¾-ounce) jar fat-free spaghetti sauce with mushrooms
9 cooked lasagna noodles (cooked without salt or fat)
2 cups (8 ounces) shredded part-skim mozzarella cheese
¼ cup plus 2 tablespoons grated Parmesan cheese

1 Combine first 3 ingredients in a medium bowl; stir well, and set aside.

2 Spread ½ cup spaghetti sauce in a 13- x 9- x 2-inch baking dish. Place 3 noodles over sauce; spoon one-third of spinach mixture over noodles. Top with one-third of remaining spaghetti sauce, ½ cup mozzarella cheese, and 2 tablespoons Parmesan cheese. Repeat procedure twice with remaining noodles, spinach mixture, spaghetti sauce, 1 cup mozzarella, and remaining Parmesan cheese. Top with remaining ½ cup mozzarella cheese. Bake, uncovered, at 350° for 30 to 35 minutes or until thoroughly heated. Let stand 10 minutes.
Yield: 8 servings.

Per Serving: Calories 278 (22% from fat)   Fat 6.9g (Sat 4.1g)   Protein 23.6g
Carbohydrate 30.2g   Fiber 3.6g   Cholesterol 22mg   Sodium 803mg

Sun-Dried Tomato Pizza

Prep: 21 minutes   Cook: 8 minutes

12 sun-dried tomatoes (packed without oil)
¾ cup boiling water
3 cloves garlic
¼ cup coarsely chopped fresh basil
¼ cup coarsely chopped fresh parsley
⅛ teaspoon pepper
¾ cup light process cream cheese, softened
1 (10-ounce) thin-crust Italian bread shell (such as Boboli)
3 tablespoons freshly grated Parmesan cheese

1 Combine tomatoes and boiling water; let stand 10 minutes. Drain. Position knife blade in food processor bowl. Drop garlic through food chute with processor running; process 3 seconds. Add basil, parsley, and pepper; process until herb mixture is minced. Add tomatoes, one at a time, through food chute; process until minced.

2 Spread cream cheese over bread shell. Sprinkle tomato mixture over cream cheese, covering cheese completely. Place on an ungreased baking sheet. Bake at 450° for 5 minutes; sprinkle with Parmesan cheese. Bake 3 additional minutes or until cheese melts.
Yield: 4 servings.

Per Serving: Calories 310 (37% from fat)   Fat 12.7g (Sat 6.2g)   Protein 15.4g
Carbohydrate 34.6g   Fiber 1.3g   Cholesterol 34mg   Sodium 745mg

■ Sun-dried tomatoes provide a more intense tomato flavor than fresh, and they are easy to keep on hand. An unopened package can be stored in the pantry up to one year; an opened package will keep for three months. To use them, pour boiling water over the tomatoes and let them stand for 10 minutes.

*Sun-Dried
Tomato Pizza*

Stuffed Poblanos

Prep: 40 minutes   Cook: 20 minutes

Cut a strip from the long side of each pepper.

Chop enough of the pepper strips to get ½ cup chopped pepper.

10 large poblano peppers
1 (7½-ounce) package pinto beans and rice mix
1 cup frozen whole-kernel corn, thawed
1 cup (4 ounces) shredded reduced-fat Monterey Jack cheese
1 tablespoon taco seasoning mix
1 (15-ounce) can no-salt-added crushed tomatoes, undrained
1 (15½-ounce) jar no-salt-added mild salsa

1 Cut a lengthwise strip from each pepper. Chop enough of pepper strips to measure ½ cup; reserve remaining strips for another use. Remove and discard seeds from peppers. Cook peppers in boiling water to cover 5 minutes; drain and set aside.

2 Cook bean mix according to package directions, omitting fat and seasoning packet. Combine chopped pepper, bean mix, corn, and next 3 ingredients. Spoon evenly into peppers; place peppers in a 13- x 9- x 2-inch baking dish. Add hot water to dish to a depth of ¼ inch. Bake at 350° for 20 minutes or until thoroughly heated.

3 Position knife blade in food processor bowl; add salsa. Process until smooth. Spoon salsa onto plates; top with peppers.
Yield: 5 servings (serving size: 2 stuffed peppers plus salsa).

Per Serving: Calories 335 (14% from fat)   Fat 5.3g (Sat 2.6g)   Protein 17.2g
Carbohydrate 56.8g   Fiber 6.0g   Cholesterol 15mg   Sodium 548mg

Stuffed Poblanos

Risotto with Peas and Peppers

Prep: 15 minutes   Cook: 30 minutes

1 (14½-ounce) can vegetable broth
2¾ cups water
Vegetable cooking spray
1 cup plus 2 tablespoons Arborio rice, uncooked
¼ cup diced dried tomato (packed without oil)
⅔ cup frozen English peas, thawed
⅔ cup freshly grated Parmesan cheese
⅓ cup commercial roasted red pepper, drained and chopped
1 teaspoon dried Italian seasoning
½ teaspoon pepper

1 Combine broth and water in a medium saucepan; place over medium heat. Cover and bring to a simmer; reduce heat to low, and keep warm. (Do not boil.)

2 Coat a large saucepan with cooking spray; place over medium-low heat until hot. Add rice and 1 cup simmering broth mixture. Cook, stirring constantly, until most of liquid is absorbed. Add 1½ cups broth mixture, ½ cup at a time, cooking and stirring constantly until each ½ cup addition is absorbed. Stir in tomato. Add remaining 2 cups broth mixture, ½ cup at a time, cooking and stirring constantly until each ½ cup addition is absorbed. (Rice will be tender and will have a creamy consistency.) Add peas and remaining ingredients, stirring until cheese melts; serve immediately.
Yield: 4 (1-cup) servings.

Per Serving: Calories 303 (14% from fat)   Fat 4.7g (Sat 2.3g)   Protein 10.6g
Carbohydrate 54.0g   Fiber 3.0g   Cholesterol 9mg   Sodium 857mg

■ Risotto is an Italian rice dish made with short-grain Arborio rice. As you cook the rice, keep adding simmering liquid so that it will be thick and creamy.

$\mathcal{M}$eats

Meat, whether it be beef, pork, or lamb, can be simply wonderful when simply cooked. Roasting, for example, is one of the easiest and most basic cooking methods for meats. There's no need to fuss. All you have to do is brush on a little oil, sprinkle some herbs on top, and place the meat in the oven.

I like to toss in some vegetables to roast along with the meat so that my whole meal is done when I wake up from my nap.

Roasted Lamb and Vegetables (page 141)

123

Sometimes you *can* please everybody. This sandwich tastes like a taco, but looks like a hamburger. And you can have it on the table quicker than you can go to a fast-food drive-through.

Taco Burgers

Prep: 10 minutes   Cook: 10 minutes

¾ **pound ground round**
½ **cup enchilada sauce (or salsa), divided**
Vegetable cooking spray
½ **cup canned fat-free refried beans**
4 **reduced-calorie whole wheat hamburger buns**
1 **cup shredded lettuce**
½ **cup chopped tomato**
½ **cup (2 ounces) shredded reduced-fat sharp Cheddar cheese**

1 Combine meat and ¼ cup enchilada sauce. Shape meat mixture into 4 (½-inch-thick) patties. Coat a nonstick skillet with cooking spray. Place over medium heat until hot. Add patties, and cook 4 to 5 minutes on each side or until done. Remove from skillet; drain on paper towels.

2 Spread 2 tablespoons refried beans on bottom half of each bun. Top each with ¼ cup shredded lettuce, 2 tablespoons chopped tomato, and 2 tablespoons shredded cheese. Top each with a meat patty. Spoon remaining ¼ cup enchilada sauce evenly over patties. Top with remaining bun halves.
Yield: 4 servings.

Per Serving: Calories 296 (29% from fat)   Fat 9.6g (Sat 3.4g)   Protein 26.2g   Carbohydrate 24.1g   Fiber 3.4g   Cholesterol 62mg   Sodium 567mg

Taco Burger

For easy clean-up, line the bottom of the broiler pan with heavy-duty aluminum foil. Then all you'll have to do is throw away the foil.

Barbecue Meat Loaf

Prep: 6 minutes   Cook: 1 hour and 20 minutes

2 slices whole wheat bread, torn into pieces
1 cup frozen chopped onion, celery, and pepper blend, thawed
1½ pounds ground round
½ cup 1% low-fat milk
½ cup egg substitute
1 teaspoon minced garlic
¼ teaspoon salt
¼ teaspoon pepper
Vegetable cooking spray
½ cup fat-free barbecue sauce

1 Position knife blade in food processor bowl. Add bread and vegetable blend to processor bowl; process until chopped. Add meat and next 5 ingredients. Pulse until combined.

2 Shape meat mixture into an 8- x 4-inch loaf; place on a rack in a roasting pan coated with cooking spray. Bake at 350° for 1 hour and 10 minutes. Spread barbecue sauce over meat loaf. Bake 10 minutes. **Yield: 8 servings.**

Per Serving: Calories 178 (24% from fat)   Fat 4.7g (Sat 1.7g)   Protein 21.9g   Carbohydrate 11.0g   Fiber 0.3g   Cholesterol 50mg   Sodium 383mg

A cubed beef steak is not really in cubes, but is a steak taken from top or bottom round and tenderized (or cubed) by running it through a butcher's tenderizing machine.

Lemon-Herb Cubed Steaks

Prep: 10 minutes   Cook: 16 minutes

1 cup fine, dry breadcrumbs
¼ cup grated Parmesan cheese
½ teaspoon dried Italian seasoning
¼ teaspoon salt
¼ teaspoon freshly ground pepper
3 egg whites, lightly beaten
1 teaspoon grated lemon rind
2 tablespoons fresh lemon juice
4 (4-ounce) cubed beef steaks
Olive oil-flavored vegetable cooking spray

1 Combine first 5 ingredients. Combine egg whites, rind, and juice. Dip steaks into egg white mixture; dredge in breadcrumb mixture. Coat a nonstick skillet with cooking spray; place over medium heat. Add steaks; cook 8 minutes on each side or until tender. **Yield: 4 servings.**

Per Serving: Calories 297 (24% from fat)   Fat 8.0g (Sat 3.1g)   Protein 32.8g   Carbohydrate 21.5g   Fiber 1.2g   Cholesterol 65mg   Sodium 578mg

Smothered Steak

Prep: 10 minutes   Cook: 8 hours

1   (1½-pound) lean boneless round tip steak
3   tablespoons all-purpose flour
¼   teaspoon pepper
1   (14½-ounce) can no-salt-added stewed tomatoes, undrained
1   (10-ounce) package frozen chopped onion, celery, and pepper
        blend, thawed
3   tablespoons low-sodium Worcestershire sauce
1   tablespoon red wine vinegar
¼   teaspoon salt
3   cups cooked long-grain rice (cooked without salt or fat)

1 Trim fat from steak; cut steak into 1½-inch pieces. Place steak in a 4-quart electric slow cooker. Add flour and pepper; toss. Add tomato and next 4 ingredients; stir well. Cover and cook on low setting 8 hours or until steak is tender, stirring once. Spoon over rice.
Yield: 6 servings.

Per Serving: Calories 312 (15% from fat)   Fat 5.1g (Sat 1.8g)   Protein 27.9g
Carbohydrate 36.5g   Fiber 0.6g   Cholesterol 68mg   Sodium 225mg

■ Electric slow cookers are making a comeback in today's kitchens. Using one is like having a personal chef, but cheaper. Just throw some ingredients into the pot, go to work, and come home to a hot meal.

Simple Beef Stroganoff

Prep: 10 minutes   Cook: 10 minutes

¾   pound lean boneless top sirloin steak
Vegetable cooking spray
½   cup sliced onion
1   pound fresh mushrooms, sliced
¼   cup dry white wine
¼   teaspoon salt
¼   teaspoon freshly ground pepper
1   (10¾-ounce) can reduced-fat, reduced-sodium cream
        of mushroom soup
½   cup nonfat sour cream
4½   cups cooked egg noodles (cooked without salt or fat)

1 Trim fat from steak; cut steak into thin slices. Coat a nonstick skillet with cooking spray; place over medium-high heat until hot. Add steak; sauté 5 minutes. Add onion and mushrooms; sauté 5 minutes. Reduce heat to medium-low. Add wine, salt, and pepper; cook 2 minutes. Combine soup and sour cream; stir into steak mixture. Cook until thoroughly heated. Serve over noodles.
Yield: 6 servings.

Per Serving: Calories 307 (18% from fat)   Fat 6.3g (Sat 1.9g)   Protein 21.7g
Carbohydrate 40.2g   Fiber 4.1g   Cholesterol 78mg   Sodium 357mg

■ Cook the noodles while you're cooking the meat mixture so that everything's ready at the same time.

To serve the grilled leeks, cut them in half lengthwise, or cut them crosswise into rounds. If you want to grill limes for a garnish, cut them in slices or wedges, and add them to the grill along with the steaks and leeks. Grill about 10 minutes, turning once.

Glazed Sirloin with Leeks

Prep: 10 minutes   Cook: 10 minutes

2 (1-pound) lean boneless top sirloin steaks (½ inch thick)
½ teaspoon salt
¼ teaspoon pepper
8 medium leeks
½ cup no-sugar-added peach spread
¼ cup plus 2 tablespoons honey mustard
1 tablespoon fresh lime juice
2 teaspoons olive oil
¼ teaspoon ground coriander
Vegetable cooking spray
Fresh cilantro leaves (optional)
Fresh lime and peach slices (optional)

1 Sprinkle steaks with salt and pepper; set aside. Remove and discard roots, tough outer leaves, and tops from leeks, leaving 2 inches of dark leaves. Set aside.

2 Combine peach spread and next 4 ingredients in a glass measure. Microwave at HIGH 1 minute; set aside half of mixture.

3 Coat grill rack with cooking spray; place on grill over medium coals (300° to 350°). Place steaks and leeks on rack; grill, covered, 5 minutes on each side or until steaks are desired degree of doneness, basting often with half of peach mixture. Serve with reserved peach mixture. If desired, garnish with cilantro and lime and peach slices.
Yield: 8 servings.

Per Serving: Calories 294 (23% from fat)   Fat 7.6g (Sat 2.6g)   Protein 27.2g
Carbohydrate 28.0g   Fiber 1.1g   Cholesterol 76mg   Sodium 262mg

*Glazed Sirloin
with Leeks*

Jalapeño Beef Kabobs

Prep: 17 minutes   Marinate: 30 minutes   Cook: 12 minutes

1 (1½-pound) sirloin tip steak
¾ cup fat-free red wine vinaigrette, divided
12 medium-size fresh mushrooms
6 medium jalapeño peppers
2 medium-size yellow squash, cut into ½-inch pieces
1 medium-size purple onion, cut into 12 wedges
¼ cup hot jalapeño jelly
Vegetable cooking spray

1 Trim fat from steak; cut steak into 1-inch pieces. Place steak in a heavy-duty, zip-top plastic bag. Add ½ cup vinaigrette. Seal bag; shake until steak is coated. Marinate in refrigerator 30 minutes, turning bag once. Remove steak from marinade; discard marinade. Thread steak and vegetables alternately on 6 (15-inch) skewers.

2 Combine remaining ¼ cup vinaigrette and jelly in a small saucepan. Cook over low heat, stirring constantly, until jelly melts.

3 Coat grill rack with cooking spray; place on grill over medium-hot coals (350° to 400°). Place kabobs on rack; grill, covered, 6 minutes on each side or until steak is desired degree of doneness, basting often with jelly mixture.
Yield: 6 servings.

Per Serving: Calories 327 (18% from fat)   Fat 6.6g (Sat 2.4g)   Protein 28.1g
Carbohydrate 26.8g   Fiber 2.5g   Cholesterol 76mg   Sodium 293mg

■ Some like it hot and some don't! For timid tastebuds, use 1 small green pepper cut into 1-inch pieces instead of 6 whole jalapeños.

Allspice is a dark brown pea-size berry that comes from an evergreen pimiento tree. It's called allspice because it tastes like a combination of cinnamon, nutmeg, and cloves.

Jamaican Peppered Steak

Prep: 7 minutes   Cook: 22 minutes

1   (1-pound) lean boneless beef tenderloin
1   tablespoon whole allspice, crushed
1½   teaspoons black peppercorns, crushed
Vegetable cooking spray
1   tablespoon all-purpose flour
2   tablespoons water
1   cup canned no-salt-added beef broth
3   tablespoons Grand Marnier or other orange-flavored liqueur
½   cup evaporated skimmed milk
¼   teaspoon salt

1 Trim fat from tenderloin; cut tenderloin into 4 equal pieces. Sprinkle tenderloin evenly with crushed allspice and peppercorns.

2 Coat a nonstick skillet with cooking spray; place over medium-high heat until hot. Add tenderloin; cook 3 to 5 minutes on each side or to desired degree of doneness. Remove from skillet; set aside, and keep warm. Wipe drippings from skillet with a paper towel.

3 Combine flour and water in a small bowl, stirring with a wire whisk until smooth. Combine broth and remaining 3 ingredients in skillet. Stir in flour mixture. Bring to a boil, stirring constantly. Reduce heat, and simmer, stirring constantly, 12 minutes or until thickened. Spoon gravy over tenderloin.
Yield: 4 servings.

Per Serving: Calories 221 (35% from fat)   Fat 8.5g (Sat 3.2g)   Protein 27.0g Carbohydrate 7.4g   Fiber 0.6g   Cholesterol 73mg   Sodium 241mg

Roasted Reuben Tenderloin

Prep: 27 minutes   Cook: 50 minutes

Vegetable cooking spray
½ cup chopped red cooking apple
½ cup chopped onion
⅛ teaspoon ground allspice
1½ cups sauerkraut, well drained
1 (3-pound) beef tenderloin
¼ cup plus 2 tablespoons fat-free Thousand Island dressing,
     divided
½ teaspoon coarsely ground pepper
2 cups soft rye breadcrumbs

1 Coat a large nonstick skillet with cooking spray; place over medium-high heat until hot. Add apple, onion, and allspice; sauté until onion is tender. Remove from heat; stir in sauerkraut. Set aside.

2 Trim fat from tenderloin. Cut tenderloin lengthwise down center, cutting to, but not through, bottom. Flip cut piece out to enlarge tenderloin. Brush ¼ cup dressing over cut surface of meat. Spoon sauerkraut mixture over dressing. Bring sides of meat together, and tie securely at 2-inch intervals using heavy string. Brush remaining 2 tablespoons dressing over tenderloin. Sprinkle tenderloin with pepper, and roll in breadcrumbs. Place, seam side down, on a rack in a roasting pan coated with cooking spray. Insert meat thermometer into thickest part of tenderloin, if desired.

3 Bake, uncovered, at 425° for 50 to 60 minutes or until meat thermometer registers 145° (medium-rare) or 160° (medium). Cover with aluminum foil the last 25 minutes of baking to prevent excessive browning, if necessary. Remove tenderloin from oven, and let stand 10 minutes. Cut into ½-inch-thick slices.
Yield: 12 servings.

Per Serving: Calories 219 (32% from fat)   Fat 7.8g (Sat 3.0g)   Protein 25.1g
Carbohydrate 10.9g   Fiber 1.8g   Cholesterol 70mg   Sodium 352mg

Tie Up a Tenderloin

Cut the tenderloin lengthwise down the center, but don't cut all the way through, so that one long side will be connected.

Spoon the sauerkraut mixture onto the meat after you have brushed the meat with dressing.

Bring two sides of the meat together, and tie securely with heavy string to keep the filling inside the meat.

Gourmet Grilled Pizzas

Prep: 15 minutes   **Cook:** 13 minutes

1 small fennel bulb (about ½ pound)
1 (1-pound) beef tenderloin
¼ teaspoon salt
¼ teaspoon freshly ground pepper
Vegetable cooking spray
1 (6-ounce) package sliced fresh portobello mushrooms
4 (6-inch) focaccia rounds
½ cup tomato chutney
2 ounces thinly sliced fontina cheese

1 Trim tough outer stalks from fennel. Cut bulb in half lengthwise; remove and discard core. Set bulb aside.

2 Cut tenderloin lengthwise down center, cutting to, but not through, bottom. Flip cut piece over to enlarge tenderloin, and sprinkle with salt and pepper.

3 Coat grill rack with cooking spray; place on grill over medium-hot coals (350° to 400°). Place tenderloin and fennel on rack; grill, covered, 5 minutes. Add mushrooms. Grill 5 additional minutes or until tenderloin is desired degree of doneness and vegetables are tender, turning tenderloin and vegetables once. Cut tenderloin and fennel into thin slices.

4 Arrange tenderloin, fennel, and mushrooms evenly over focaccia rounds. Spoon 2 tablespoons chutney over each round; top with cheese. Return to grill rack; grill 3 minutes or until cheese melts.
Yield: 4 servings.

Per Serving: Calories 363 (34% from fat)   Fat 13.7g (Sat 6.3g)   Protein 31.9g   Carbohydrate 28.7g   Fiber 2.3g   Cholesterol 88mg   Sodium 357mg

Pizza Pizzazz

Go one step beyond pepperoni and combine these out-of-the-ordinary ingredients for pizzas with extraordinary flavor:

Fennel: a pale green plant with celerylike stems, bright green leaves, and a broad bulb that's treated like a vegetable.
Portobello Mushrooms: large, round, flat mushrooms with a meaty flavor. (See photo on page 92.)
Focaccia: Italian flat bread rounds now available in grocery stores in packages of one or two.
Tomato Chutney: a spicy condiment with chunks of tomato, vinegar, and sugar.
Fontina: a mild, semi-firm Italian cheese with a golden brown rind and a pale yellow interior.

Gourmet Grilled Pizza

The pan juices and dried fruit blend together to make a rich gravy. The roast with its gravy is wonderful served with baked or mashed sweet potatoes.

Fruited Cider Roast

Prep: 20 minutes   Cook: 3 hours

1 (3½-pound) lean boneless top round roast
¼ teaspoon salt
¼ teaspoon pepper
Vegetable cooking spray
6 cups unsweetened apple cider
3 cups cider vinegar
1 (6-ounce) package dried apricot halves, chopped
½ cup raisins
¼ cup firmly packed dark brown sugar
¼ teaspoon ground allspice

1 Trim fat from roast. Sprinkle roast with salt and pepper. Coat a large Dutch oven with cooking spray; place over medium-high heat until hot. Add roast, and cook until browned on all sides.

2 Combine cider and vinegar; pour over roast. Bring to a boil; cover, reduce heat, and simmer 3 to 3½ hours or until roast is tender. Transfer roast to a serving platter; set aside, and keep warm.

3 Skim fat from pan juices. Reserve 2 cups juices; discard remaining juices. Return 2 cups juices to Dutch oven; add apricot and remaining 3 ingredients. Cook over medium-high heat 8 to 10 minutes or until thickened, stirring often. Serve fruit mixture with roast.
Yield: 12 servings.

Per Serving: Calories 253 (20% from fat)   Fat 5.6g (Sat 1.9g)   Protein 28.4g
Carbohydrate 22.5g   Fiber 1.5g   Cholesterol 73mg   Sodium 107mg

Roast with Peppered Gravy

Prep: 10 minutes   Cook: 1 hour

1   (2-pound) lean boneless eye of round roast
Vegetable cooking spray
1   medium onion, cut into wedges
1¼ cups canned no-salt-added beef broth
¼   cup red wine vinegar
1   teaspoon dried crushed red pepper
½   teaspoon salt
¼   teaspoon pepper
2   large cloves garlic, crushed
3   tablespoons all-purpose flour
2   tablespoons water

1 Trim fat from roast. Coat a 4-quart pressure cooker with cooking spray; place over medium-high heat until hot. Add roast; cook until browned on all sides. Add onion and next 6 ingredients. Cover cooker with lid, and seal securely. Place pressure control over vent and tube. Cook over high heat until pressure control rocks back and forth quickly. Reduce heat until pressure control rocks occasionally; cook 40 minutes.

2 Run cold water over pressure cooker to reduce pressure rapidly. Carefully remove lid so that steam escapes away from you. Transfer roast to a serving platter; set aside, and keep warm.

3 Skim fat from pan juices. Combine flour and water, stirring until smooth; add flour mixture to juices. Cook over medium heat, stirring constantly, until thickened. Serve gravy with roast.
Yield: 8 servings.

Per Serving: Calories 176 (28% from fat)   Fat 5.5g (Sat 2.0g)   Protein 24.4g
Carbohydrate 5.2g   Fiber 0.6g   Cholesterol 56mg   Sodium 200mg

■ There's no need to be afraid of a pressure cooker. It's an ideal way to cook a large piece of meat in a short amount of time. The pressurized steam tenderizes lean cuts of meat like eye of round.

Osso Buco

Osso Buco

Prep: 18 minutes   Cook: 1 hour

4 (5-ounce) veal shanks
2 tablespoons all-purpose flour
Olive oil-flavored vegetable cooking spray
½ cup chopped onion
½ cup chopped carrot
2 (14½-ounce) cans no-salt-added diced tomatoes, undrained
½ cup dry white wine
½ cup canned no-salt-added beef broth
½ teaspoon salt
¼ teaspoon freshly ground pepper
1½ teaspoons minced fresh parsley (optional)
1½ teaspoons grated lemon rind (optional)
1½ teaspoons minced garlic (optional)

1 Trim fat from veal shanks; dredge shanks in flour. Coat a Dutch oven with cooking spray; place over medium-high heat until hot. Add shanks; cook until browned on all sides. Remove shanks; set aside, and keep warm. Wipe drippings from Dutch oven with a paper towel.

2 Coat Dutch oven with cooking spray; place over medium-high heat until hot. Add onion and carrot, and sauté until tender. Stir in tomato and next 4 ingredients; add shanks. Bring to a boil; cover, reduce heat, and simmer 20 minutes. Uncover and simmer 30 additional minutes or until shanks are tender.

3 Transfer each veal shank to an individual soup bowl; spoon vegetable mixture over meat. If desired, combine parsley, lemon rind, and garlic, and sprinkle evenly over each serving.
Yield: 4 servings.

Per Serving: Calories 220 (16% from fat)   Fat 3.8g (Sat 1.0g)   Protein 25.6g   Carbohydrate 20.4g   Fiber 2.4g   Cholesterol 98mg   Sodium 443mg

Osso buco is a traditional Italian dish of veal shanks and tomatoes. When you're in-the-know, you garnish it with gremolata (a mixture of minced parsley, lemon rind, and garlic).

Zest (the colored outer portion of the skin of citrus fruits) makes an easy garnish. Use a grater, vegetable peeler, or small sharp knife to make the threadlike strips of citrus peel. Or you can purchase a zesting tool to remove the zest.

Veal in Lime Cream Sauce

Prep: 13 minutes   Cook: 10 minutes

1 pound veal cutlets (¼ inch thick)
¼ teaspoon salt
¼ teaspoon freshly ground pepper
Butter-flavored vegetable cooking spray
2 tablespoons fresh lime juice
2 tablespoons dry white wine
1 tablespoon plus 1 teaspoon all-purpose flour
½ cup canned low-sodium chicken broth
⅔ cup evaporated skimmed milk
½ teaspoon lime zest

1 Sprinkle veal cutlets with salt and pepper. Coat a large nonstick skillet with cooking spray; place over medium-high heat until hot. Add cutlets, and cook 1 minute on each side or until browned. Remove from skillet; set aside, and keep warm.

2 Add lime juice and wine to skillet; cook over high heat 1 minute or until mixture is reduced by half. Combine flour, broth, and milk; stir well. Add to lime juice mixture. Cook over medium heat, stirring constantly, 5 minutes or until thickened and bubbly. Return cutlets to skillet; cook until thoroughly heated. Transfer to a serving platter. Sprinkle with lime zest, and serve immediately.
Yield: 4 servings.

Per Serving: Calories 218 (25% from fat)   Fat 6.1g (Sat 1.6g)   Protein 31.0g
Carbohydrate 8.1g   Fiber 0.1g   Cholesterol 102mg   Sodium 282mg

Veal in Lime Cream Sauce

Veal Chops with Wild Mushrooms

Prep: 18 minutes   Cook: 30 minutes

Vegetable cooking spray
4 (6-ounce) lean veal loin chops (¾ inch thick)
½ cup fresh shiitake mushrooms, thinly sliced
½ cup fresh oyster mushrooms, thinly sliced
1 cup canned no-salt-added chicken broth
½ cup evaporated skimmed milk
¼ cup (1 ounce) shredded reduced-fat Swiss cheese
1 teaspoon minced fresh thyme

1 Coat a large nonstick skillet with cooking spray; place over medium heat until hot. Add veal chops; cook 2 to 3 minutes on each side or until browned. Remove chops from skillet. Drain and pat dry with paper towels. Set chops aside. Wipe drippings from skillet with a paper towel.

2 Coat skillet with cooking spray; place over medium-high heat until hot. Add mushrooms; sauté until tender. Remove mushrooms from skillet; set aside.

3 Return chops to skillet; pour broth over chops. Bring to a boil; cover, reduce heat, and simmer 20 to 25 minutes or until chops are tender. Remove chops from skillet; set aside, and keep warm.

4 Add milk to liquid in skillet. Bring to a boil; cook, stirring constantly, 1 minute or until thickened. Stir in mushrooms, cheese, and thyme. Cook, stirring constantly, until cheese melts. Spoon sauce evenly over chops. Serve immediately.
Yield: 4 servings.

Per Serving: Calories 199 (27% from fat)   Fat 6.0g (Sat 1.9g)   Protein 28.6g
Carbohydrate 6.2g   Fiber 0.4g   Cholesterol 96mg   Sodium 186mg

■ The shiitake and oyster mushrooms add a robust flavor to the veal, but if you're not in a wild mood, mushroomwise, that is, use 1 cup of regular sliced mushrooms.

Traditional Greek moussaka has layers of eggplant and ground lamb topped with a thick, creamy white sauce. It's easier to top it with a can of cream of mushroom soup.

Moussaka

Prep: 45 minutes   Cook: 25 minutes

2 small eggplants (about ¾ pound each)
Olive-oil flavored vegetable cooking spray
1 pound lean ground lamb (or ground round)
1 (27½-ounce) jar fat-free chunky spaghetti sauce with mushrooms
1 teaspoon ground cinnamon
½ teaspoon pepper
1 (10¾-ounce) can reduced-fat, reduced-sodium cream of
       mushroom soup
⅓ cup water
2 tablespoons fine, dry breadcrumbs
2 tablespoons freshly grated Parmesan cheese

1 Peel eggplants, and cut crosswise into ¼-inch-thick slices. Place on a large baking sheet coated with cooking spray. Coat slices with cooking spray. Bake at 375° for 25 minutes or until eggplant is tender and lightly browned, turning once. Let cool slightly.

2 Coat a large nonstick skillet with cooking spray; place over medium-high heat until hot. Add meat, and cook until browned, stirring until it crumbles. Drain and pat dry with paper towels. Wipe drippings from skillet with a paper towel.

3 Return meat to skillet; add spaghetti sauce, cinnamon, and pepper. Bring to a boil; reduce heat, and simmer, uncovered, 5 minutes or until meat mixture is thickened, stirring occasionally.

4 Coat an 11- x 7- x 1½-inch baking dish with cooking spray; place half of eggplant slices in dish; top with half of meat mixture. Repeat layers with remaining eggplant slices and remaining meat mixture. Combine soup and water in a medium bowl, stirring until smooth; pour over meat mixture. Combine breadcrumbs and cheese in a small bowl. Sprinkle crumb mixture over soup mixture. Bake, uncovered, at 375° for 25 minutes or until browned and bubbly.
Yield: 6 servings.

Per Serving: Calories 248 (28% from fat)   Fat 7.8g (Sat 2.7g)   Protein 22.9g   Carbohydrate 23.3g   Fiber 4.2g   Cholesterol 59mg   Sodium 685mg

Roasted Lamb and Vegetables

Prep: 25 minutes   Cook: 2 hours and 10 minutes

1 (3½-pound) lean boneless leg of lamb
7 large cloves garlic, sliced
2 tablespoons chopped fresh rosemary
1 teaspoon salt
1 teaspoon freshly ground pepper
Olive oil-flavored vegetable cooking spray
2¾ pounds small round red potatoes
2 (1-pound) packages baby carrots
1 (14¼-ounce) can no-salt-added beef broth
¼ cup water
2 tablespoons cornstarch
Fresh rosemary sprigs (optional)

1 Trim fat from lamb. Make ¼-inch-deep slits in lamb; insert a garlic slice into each slit. Combine chopped rosemary, salt, and pepper. Sprinkle half of rosemary mixture over lamb. Insert meat thermometer into thickest part of lamb, if desired. Place lamb in a large roasting pan coated with cooking spray; add potatoes, carrots, and beef broth.

2 Sprinkle vegetables with remaining rosemary mixture. Bake, uncovered, at 350° for 2 hours or until meat thermometer registers 150° (medium-rare) to 160° (medium), stirring vegetables occasionally.

3 Transfer lamb to a serving platter; arrange vegetables around lamb, and keep warm. Skim fat from pan juices. Combine ¼ cup water and cornstarch, stirring until smooth. Add cornstarch mixture to pan juices, stirring with a wire whisk. Bring to a boil over medium heat, stirring constantly. Cook, stirring constantly, until thickened and bubbly. Serve gravy with lamb and vegetables. Garnish with rosemary sprigs, if desired.
Yield: 14 servings. *(Recipe pictured on page 122.)*

Per Serving: Calories 267 (23% from fat)   Fat 6.9g (Sat 2.4g)   Protein 26.9g
Carbohydrate 23.3g   Fiber 3.8g   Cholesterol 76mg   Sodium 256mg

■ Be sure to ask the butcher for a leg of lamb that has been well trimmed of excess fat.

■ Slice yellow squash, zucchini, and red peppers in half and toss on the grill along with the pork. Grill the vegetables until they're tender (about 8 to 10 minutes), and coarsely chop for a colorful, easy side dish.

Tenderloins with Cream Sauce

Prep: 12 minutes   Cook: 25 minutes

Vegetable cooking spray
2 (¾-pound) pork tenderloins
¾ cup 1% low-fat milk
1½ tablespoons all-purpose flour, divided
3 tablespoons Dijon mustard
2 tablespoons dry white wine
¼ cup nonfat sour cream
⅛ teaspoon pepper
Fresh rosemary sprigs (optional)

1 Coat grill rack with cooking spray; place on grill over medium-hot coals (350° to 400°). Insert meat thermometer into thickest part of one tenderloin, if desired. Place tenderloins on rack. Grill, covered, 25 to 30 minutes or until meat thermometer registers 160°, turning occasionally.

2 Combine milk and 1 tablespoon flour in a saucepan, stirring until smooth. Cook over medium heat, stirring constantly, until thickened. Stir in mustard and wine; remove from heat. Combine remaining 1½ teaspoons flour and sour cream; add to milk mixture, stirring well. Stir in pepper. Serve with tenderloins. Garnish with rosemary, if desired. **Yield: 6 servings.**

Per Serving: Calories 188 (25% from fat)   Fat 5.3g (Sat 1.7g)   Protein 28.1g Carbohydrate 4.3g   Fiber 0.1g   Cholesterol 86mg   Sodium 307mg

Tenderloin with Cream Sauce

Quick Pork Parmesan

Prep: 10 minutes   Cook: 30 minutes

4 (4-ounce) boneless center-cut pork loin chops
⅓ cup fine, dry breadcrumbs
2 tablespoons grated Parmesan cheese
¼ cup egg substitute
Vegetable cooking spray
1½ cups low-fat spaghetti sauce with garlic and herbs
½ cup (2 ounces) shredded reduced-fat mozzarella cheese

1 Trim fat from pork chops. Place chops between two sheets of heavy-duty plastic wrap, and flatten to ¼-inch thickness, using a meat mallet or rolling pin.

2 Combine breadcrumbs and Parmesan cheese in a small bowl. Dip chops in egg substitute; dredge in breadcrumb mixture.

3 Coat a large nonstick skillet with cooking spray; place over medium heat until hot. Add chops, and cook 1 to 2 minutes on each side or until browned. Arrange chops in an 8-inch square baking dish coated with cooking spray. Pour spaghetti sauce over chops. Cover and bake at 350° for 25 minutes or until chops are tender. Uncover; sprinkle with mozzarella cheese. Bake 5 additional minutes or until cheese melts. Serve immediately.
Yield: 4 servings.

Per Serving: Calories 322 (33% from fat)   Fat 11.8g (Sat 4.7g)   Protein 34.6g
Carbohydrate 17.1g   Fiber 2.0g   Cholesterol 79mg   Sodium 614mg

■ An easy substitute for the garlic-and-herb spaghetti sauce is a plain low-fat spaghetti sauce plus 1 teaspoon minced garlic.

This recipe calls for capellini (angel hair pasta), but you might prefer to use vermicelli, spaghettini, or fettuccine instead. They're all spaghetti noodles—they just have different widths.

Braised Pork Marsala

Prep: 5 minutes   Cook: 10 minutes

1 (1-pound) pork tenderloin
¼ cup all-purpose flour
⅛ teaspoon salt
1 tablespoon margarine
¾ cup Marsala wine
1 teaspoon beef-flavored bouillon granules
¼ teaspoon freshly ground pepper
3 cups cooked capellini (cooked without salt or fat)

1 Trim fat from tenderloin; cut tenderloin into ½-inch-thick slices. Combine flour and salt in a heavy-duty, zip-top plastic bag. Seal bag; shake well. Add tenderloin. Seal bag; shake until well coated.

2 Melt margarine in a nonstick skillet over medium heat. Add tenderloin; cook until browned, turning once. Remove from skillet. Add wine, bouillon granules, and pepper to skillet; bring to a boil. Reduce heat, and simmer, uncovered, 2 minutes. Return tenderloin to skillet; cover and simmer 2 minutes or until sauce is thickened. Serve over pasta. **Yield: 4 servings.**

Per Serving: Calories 340 (17% from fat)   Fat 6.6g (Sat 1.7g)   Protein 29.7g   Carbohydrate 37.6g   Fiber 1.9g   Cholesterol 74mg   Sodium 403mg

This sweet yet savory roast tastes like satay, an Indonesian skewered snack of grilled or broiled meat served with a peanut sauce.

Indonesian Pork Tenderloin

Prep: 10 minutes   Cook: 40 minutes

1 (1-pound) pork tenderloin
2 tablespoons low-sodium soy sauce
2 tablespoons reduced-fat creamy peanut butter
1 teaspoon dried crushed red pepper
2 cloves garlic, minced
Vegetable cooking spray
¼ cup pineapple preserves

1 Trim fat from tenderloin. Combine soy sauce and next 3 ingredients, stirring well. Spread soy sauce mixture over tenderloin. Place on a rack in a roasting pan coated with cooking spray. Insert meat thermometer into thickest part of tenderloin, if desired. Bake, uncovered, at 375° for 30 minutes. Brush tenderloin with preserves. Bake 10 additional minutes or until meat thermometer registers 160°, basting often with preserves. Let stand 10 minutes before slicing. **Yield: 4 servings.**   *(Pork pictured on page 18.)*

Per Serving: Calories 247 (27% from fat)   Fat 7.3g (Sat 2.0g)   Protein 26.7g   Carbohydrate 17.5g   Fiber 3.2g   Cholesterol 79mg   Sodium 327mg

Peppered Pork Roast

Prep: 15 minutes   Cook: 3 hours and 10 minutes

1 (2-pound) lean boneless pork loin roast
1½ teaspoons mixed peppercorns, crushed and divided
¾ teaspoon salt
Vegetable cooking spray
½ cup water
1 cup nonfat sour cream
2 tablespoons all-purpose flour

1 Trim fat from roast. Combine 1¼ teaspoons crushed peppercorns and salt; rub over surface of roast.

2 Coat a nonstick skillet with cooking spray; place over medium heat until hot. Add roast, and cook until browned on all sides, turning occasionally. Transfer roast to a 4-quart electric slow cooker.

3 Add water to skillet; bring to a boil. Deglaze skillet by scraping particles that cling to bottom. Pour water mixture over roast. Cover and cook on high setting 3 hours or until roast is tender. Remove roast from cooker; set aside, and keep warm.

4 Pour pan juices from cooker into a small saucepan; skim fat from juices. Bring juices to a boil. Combine sour cream and flour; add to saucepan, stirring constantly. Cook over medium-low heat, stirring constantly, until thickened and bubbly. Stir in remaining ¼ teaspoon crushed peppercorns. Serve gravy with roast.
Yield: 8 servings.

Per Serving: Calories 206 (38% from fat)   Fat 8.7g (Sat 3.0g)   Protein 25.7g
Carbohydrate 3.8g   Fiber 0.2g   Cholesterol 68mg   Sodium 313mg

■ If you plan to be away from home all day, cook the roast in an electric slow cooker on low setting for 6 to 8 hours instead of on high.

There's no need to dice potatoes when the potato people have cut them for you, put them in a bag, and called them frozen hash browns. And, unlike many other frozen potato products, the frozen hash browns don't have added fat.

Ham and Hash Brown Casserole

Prep: 20 minutes   Cook: 1 hour

3 tablespoons all-purpose flour
1¾ cups evaporated skimmed milk, divided
¾ teaspoon dry mustard
¼ teaspoon pepper
⅛ teaspoon salt
4 ounces reduced-fat loaf process cheese spread, cubed
1 (8-ounce) carton nonfat sour cream
8 ounces reduced-fat, low-salt ham, chopped
1 (32-ounce) package frozen cubed hash browns with onions
       and peppers, thawed
Vegetable cooking spray

1 Combine flour and ½ cup milk, stirring until smooth. Combine flour mixture, remaining 1¼ cups milk, mustard, pepper, and salt in a medium saucepan, stirring well. Cook over medium heat, stirring constantly, until milk mixture is thickened and bubbly. Remove from heat; add cheese, stirring until cheese melts. Stir in sour cream.

2 Combine cheese mixture, ham, and hash browns in a large bowl, stirring well. Spoon potato mixture into a 13- x 9- x 2-inch baking dish coated with cooking spray. Cover and bake at 350° for 30 minutes. Uncover and bake 30 to 35 additional minutes or until golden.
Yield: 8 servings.

Per Serving: Calories 201 (14% from fat)   Fat 3.2g (Sat 1.5g)   Protein 15.7g
Carbohydrate 27.8g   Fiber 2.1g   Cholesterol 21mg   Sodium 570mg

Orange-Glazed Ham with Sweet Potatoes

Prep: 7 minutes   Cook: 1 hour and 30 minutes

1 (2-pound) low-fat boneless cooked honey ham (such as Healthy
    Choice honey ham)
Vegetable cooking spray
¾ cup low-sugar orange marmalade
3 tablespoons brown sugar
1 tablespoon honey mustard
¼ teaspoon ground ginger
1 (15¼-ounce) can unsweetened pineapple chunks in juice
2 (15-ounce) cans sweet potatoes in light syrup, drained

1 Place ham in a shallow roasting pan coated with cooking spray.
Cover and bake at 325° for 1 hour.

2 Combine marmalade and next 3 ingredients. Uncover ham, and
brush with ⅓ cup marmalade mixture. Reserve remaining marmalade mixture.

3 Drain pineapple chunks, reserving ¼ cup juice. Reserve remaining juice for another use. Combine pineapple and sweet potatoes.
Add ¼ cup pineapple juice to reserved marmalade mixture. Pour
marmalade mixture over sweet potatoes and pineapple; toss lightly.
Arrange sweet potato mixture around ham. Bake, uncovered, 30
additional minutes or until ham and potato are thoroughly heated.
Yield: 10 servings.

Per Serving: Calories 205 (12% from fat)   Fat 2.8g (Sat 0.8g)   Protein 16.3g
Carbohydrate 27.9g   Fiber 1.5g   Cholesterol 40mg   Sodium 663mg

■ Look for small (2-pound)
low-fat hams in the meat case
of the supermarket. Larger
hams may be in the deli
section or in the meat case.

Poultry

My idea of a quick and easy chicken meal used to be a bucket of drumsticks with cartons of mashed potatoes and coleslaw. But with these poultry recipes I realized that it doesn't take much effort, time, or creativity to put great-tasting chicken on the table. I'm not talking about anything fancy, you understand—a bird, some herbs, a little salt and pepper, an oven. It's really much better than eating from a bucket.

Lemon-Herb Roasted Chicken (page 164)

Tortilla Tips

The easiest way to cut tortillas is to stack them and cut them with kitchen scissors.

Stack 3 tortillas, and cut them into strips about ½ inch wide.

Salsa Chicken

Prep: 30 minutes   Cook: 10 minutes

6 (6-inch) corn tortillas
Vegetable cooking spray
2 cups chopped cooked chicken breast (skinned before cooking and cooked without salt)
½ cup fat-free roasted garlic-flavored salsa (or regular salsa), divided
2 cups chopped onion
1 (4½-ounce) can chopped green chiles, undrained
1 cup (4 ounces) shredded reduced-fat Monterey Jack cheese
½ cup nonfat sour cream, divided

1 Cut tortillas into ½-inch-wide strips. Place strips in a single layer on an ungreased baking sheet, and coat strips with cooking spray. Bake at 350° for 10 minutes or until crisp. Let cool.

2 Combine chicken and ¼ cup salsa in a large nonstick skillet. Bring to a boil over high heat. Reduce heat to medium-high, and cook 2 minutes, stirring occasionally. Remove from skillet. Set aside, and keep warm. Wipe skillet dry with paper towels.

3 Coat skillet with cooking spray; place over medium-high heat until hot. Add onion; sauté 2 minutes. Add green chiles; sauté 2 minutes. Add cheese and ¼ cup sour cream; stir until cheese melts.

4 To serve, arrange tortilla strips evenly on individual serving plates. Top tortilla strips evenly with chicken mixture. Spoon onion mixture evenly over chicken mixture. Top each serving with 1 tablespoon of remaining salsa and 1 tablespoon of remaining sour cream.
Yield: 4 servings.

Per Serving: Calories 333 (25% from fat)   Fat 9.2g (Sat 4.0g)   Protein 35.1g   Carbohydrate 25.7g   Fiber 3.2g   Cholesterol 79mg   Sodium 531mg

Chicken with Creole Cabbage

Prep: 15 minutes   Cook: 15 minutes

4 (4-ounce) skinned, boned chicken breast halves
¼ teaspoon salt
¼ teaspoon pepper
Butter-flavored vegetable cooking spray
3 cups coarsely chopped cabbage
¼ cup water
½ teaspoon sugar
¼ teaspoon ground red pepper
⅛ teaspoon ground allspice
1 clove garlic, minced
1 (15-ounce) can tomato sauce with onion, green peppers,
    and celery

1 Sprinkle chicken with salt and ¼ teaspoon pepper. Coat a large nonstick skillet with cooking spray; place over medium-high heat until hot. Add chicken, and cook 3 to 5 minutes on each side or until browned. Remove chicken from skillet. Add cabbage and remaining 6 ingredients to skillet; stir well.

2 Place chicken over cabbage mixture. Bring to a boil; cover, reduce heat, and simmer 15 minutes or until chicken is done and cabbage is tender, stirring occasionally.
Yield: 4 servings.

Per Serving: Calories 177 (13% from fat)   Fat 2.6g (Sat 0.4g)   Protein 27.7g
Carbohydrate 10.5g   Fiber 2.1g   Cholesterol 66mg   Sodium 474mg

The tomato sauce is what makes this cabbage creole. The ground red pepper adds a spicy kick; reduce the pepper by half for a milder version.

It's easy to crush the cereal in a plastic zip-top bag with a rolling pin. You'll need about 3 cups cereal to get ¾ cup of crumbs. Or look for a package of cornflake crumbs in the baking section of your supermarket.

Italian Chicken Rolls

Prep: 15 minutes   Cook: 35 minutes

6 (4-ounce) skinned, boned chicken breast halves
¼ teaspoon salt
¼ teaspoon pepper
½ cup chopped commercial roasted red pepper
⅓ cup light process cream cheese, softened
¼ cup pesto
¾ cup crushed corn flakes cereal
3 tablespoons chopped fresh parsley
½ teaspoon paprika
Vegetable cooking spray
Fresh thyme sprigs (optional)

1 Place chicken between 2 sheets of heavy-duty plastic wrap; flatten to ¼-inch thickness, using a meat mallet or rolling pin. Sprinkle with salt and ¼ teaspoon pepper; set aside.

2 Combine red pepper, cream cheese, and pesto in a small bowl, stirring until smooth. Spread cheese mixture evenly over chicken breasts. Roll up, jellyroll fashion; secure with wooden picks.

3 Combine crushed cereal, parsley, and paprika. Dredge chicken in cereal mixture. Place in an 11- x 7- x 1½-inch baking dish coated with cooking spray. Bake, uncovered, at 350° for 35 minutes; let stand 10 minutes. Remove wooden picks from chicken, and slice each roll into 6 rounds. Garnish with thyme sprigs, if desired. **Yield: 6 servings.**

Per Serving: Calories 253 (32% from fat)   Fat 9.0g (Sat 2.6g)   Protein 29.7g
Carbohydrate 12.1g   Fiber 0.7g   Cholesterol 75mg   Sodium 506mg

Italian Chicken Roll

Pounding the chicken breasts helps tenderize them, and makes them thinner and quicker to cook.

Grilled Firecracker Chicken

Prep: 5 minutes   Marinate: 15 minutes   Cook: 10 minutes

⅓ cup no-salt-added tomato sauce
¼ cup no-sugar-added apple jelly
2 tablespoons lemon juice
⅛ teaspoon garlic powder
Dash of salt
6 slices canned jalapeño peppers
4 (4-ounce) skinned, boned chicken breast halves
Vegetable cooking spray
Fresh jalapeño pepper slices (optional)

1 Combine first 6 ingredients in container of an electric blender or food processor; cover and process until smooth.

2 Place chicken in a heavy-duty, zip-top plastic bag. Add ¼ cup tomato sauce mixture, reserving remaining tomato sauce mixture. Seal bag, and shake until chicken is well coated. Marinate in refrigerator at least 15 minutes.

3 Remove chicken from marinade, discarding marinade. Coat grill rack with cooking spray, and place on grill over medium-hot coals (350° to 400°). Place chicken on rack; grill, covered, 5 minutes on each side or until done. Serve with reserved tomato sauce mixture. Garnish with fresh jalapeño slices, if desired.
Yield: 4 servings.   *(Chicken pictured on page 16.)*

Per Serving: Calories 168 (17% from fat)   Fat 3.2g (Sat 0.9g)   Protein 26.6g
Carbohydrate 6.5g   Fiber 0.3g   Cholesterol 72mg   Sodium 128mg

Chicken in Mustard Sauce

Prep: 8 minutes   Cook: 15 minutes

½ teaspoon paprika
¼ teaspoon salt
¼ teaspoon coarsely ground pepper
4 (4-ounce) skinned, boned chicken breast halves
Vegetable cooking spray
¼ cup dry white wine
1½ tablespoons all-purpose flour
¾ cup 1% low-fat milk, divided
1 tablespoon peppercorn mustard (or regular mustard)

1 Combine first 3 ingredients; sprinkle over chicken. Coat a non-stick skillet with cooking spray; place over medium-high heat until hot. Add chicken; cook 3 to 5 minutes on each side, or until browned. Remove chicken from skillet, and set aside.

2 Add wine to skillet; deglaze by scraping particles that cling to bottom. Combine flour and ¼ cup milk, stirring until smooth; add to skillet. Stir in remaining ½ cup milk and mustard. Cook over medium heat, stirring constantly, until thickened. Return chicken to skillet. Bring to a boil; cover, reduce heat, and simmer 5 minutes or until chicken is done.
Yield: 4 servings.

Per Serving: Calories 163 (13% from fat)   Fat 2.4g (Sat 0.7g)   Protein 28.1g   Carbohydrate 5.1g   Fiber 0.2g   Cholesterol 68mg   Sodium 356mg

■ If you like a powerful mustard punch, add an extra tablespoon of mustard.

Cordon bleu means "blue ribbon" in French. This delicious casserole version of the traditional cordon bleu chicken rolls takes first place for ease and simplicity because the ingredients are layered in one dish.

Cordon Bleu Casserole

Prep: 15 minutes   Cook: 45 minutes

6 (4-ounce) skinned, boned chicken breast halves
Butter-flavored vegetable cooking spray
3 (1-ounce) slices reduced-fat, low-salt ham, cut in half
3 (1¼-ounce) slices reduced-fat Swiss cheese, cut in half
2 cups sliced fresh mushrooms
1 (10¾-ounce) can reduced-fat, reduced-sodium
     cream of mushroom soup
3 tablespoons dry sherry
1½ cups reduced-sodium chicken-flavored stuffing mix

1 Arrange chicken in a 13- x 9- x 2-inch baking dish coated with cooking spray. Top chicken with ham and cheese.

2 Coat a nonstick skillet with cooking spray; place over medium-high heat until hot. Add mushrooms; sauté until tender. Combine mushrooms, soup, and sherry. Spoon mixture over chicken. Top with stuffing mix; coat well with cooking spray. Bake at 350° for 45 minutes.
Yield: 6 servings.

Per Serving: Calories 304 (24% from fat)   Fat 8.0g (Sat 3.8g)   Protein 38.0g
Carbohydrate 20.7g   Fiber 1.4g   Cholesterol 91mg   Sodium 665mg

Fill 'er Up

Cut a 2-inch long slit in the side of each chicken breast. Make it as deep as you can without cutting all the way through the breast. Place one cheese slice in the slit.

Crispy Cheese-Filled Chicken

Prep: 19 minutes   Cook: 1 hour

4 (6-ounce) skinned chicken breast halves
3 ounces reduced-fat extra-sharp Cheddar cheese
1 tablespoon Dijon mustard
1 cup crushed corn flakes cereal
1 teaspoon salt-free spicy pepper seasoning
1 teaspoon dried parsley flakes
½ cup nonfat buttermilk
Vegetable cooking spray

1 Cut a deep 2-inch-long slit in side of meaty portion of each breast. Slice cheese into 4 equal portions; brush with mustard. Place 1 cheese slice into each slit; secure with wooden picks.

2 Combine cereal, seasoning, and parsley. Dip chicken in buttermilk; dredge in cereal mixture. Place chicken in a 13- x 9- x 2-inch baking dish coated with cooking spray. Bake at 375° for 1 hour.
Yield: 4 servings.

Per Serving: Calories 317 (17% from fat)   Fat 6.0g (Sat 2.8g)   Protein 35.8g
Carbohydrate 27.7g   Fiber 0.3g   Cholesterol 80mg   Sodium 654mg

Hungarian Chicken

Prep: 10 minutes Cook: 40 minutes

6 (6-ounce) skinned chicken breast halves
½ teaspoon salt, divided
½ teaspoon pepper, divided
Butter-flavored vegetable cooking spray
1 large sweet onion, sliced
2 cups sliced fresh mushrooms
1 medium-size sweet red pepper, seeded and cut into thin strips
½ teaspoon dried marjoram
½ cup dry vermouth
¾ cup nonfat sour cream

1 Sprinkle chicken with ¼ teaspoon salt and ¼ teaspoon pepper. Coat a nonstick skillet with cooking spray. Place over medium-high heat until hot. Add chicken to skillet, and cook 5 minutes on each side or until browned.

2 Add onion, mushrooms, and red pepper. Sprinkle with remaining ¼ teaspoon salt, ¼ teaspoon pepper, and marjoram; add vermouth. Bring to a boil; cover, reduce heat, and simmer 10 minutes. Stir in sour cream; cover and cook 5 additional minutes. Uncover and cook 10 minutes or until chicken is done and sour cream mixture is slightly thickened, stirring occasionally.
Yield: 6 servings.

Per Serving: Calories 184 (9% from fat)   Fat 1.8g (Sat 0.4g)   Protein 29.6g
Carbohydrate 10.3g   Fiber 1.8g   Cholesterol 66mg   Sodium 294mg

■ If you don't want to use vermouth, add ½ cup white wine or ½ cup no-salt-added chicken broth instead.

The frozen food section of the grocery store is brimming with convenience products such as frozen vegetable combinations. Pick up a bag or two, and you get a mix of three or four vegetables without having to peel and chop them.

Citrus Chicken with Roasted Corn Relish

Prep: 10 minutes Marinate: 1 hour Cook: 40 minutes

4 (6-ounce) skinned chicken breast halves
⅔ cup fresh lime juice, divided
½ teaspoon ground cumin
½ teaspoon chili powder
¼ teaspoon salt
¼ teaspoon ground red pepper, divided
Olive oil-flavored vegetable cooking spray
1 (16-ounce) package frozen corn with peppers and onions, thawed
2 tablespoons chopped fresh cilantro
Fresh cilantro sprigs (optional)

1 Place chicken in a heavy-duty, zip-top plastic bag. Reserve 1 tablespoon lime juice; pour remaining juice over chicken. Seal bag, and shake until chicken is well coated. Marinate in refrigerator 1 hour, turning bag occasionally.

2 Combine cumin, chili powder, salt, and ⅛ teaspoon red pepper in a small bowl. Remove chicken from marinade, discarding marinade. Sprinkle chicken with cumin mixture.

3 Coat rack of a broiler pan with cooking spray. Place chicken, skinned sides down, on rack; broil 8 inches from heat (with electric oven door partially opened) 25 minutes. Turn chicken, and broil 15 additional minutes or until done. Set chicken aside, and keep warm.

4 Coat a large nonstick skillet with cooking spray. Place skillet over medium-high heat until hot. Add corn mixture and remaining ⅛ teaspoon red pepper; sauté until corn is lightly browned and tender. Spoon corn evenly onto individual serving plates; top each serving with chicken. Drizzle evenly with reserved 1 tablespoon lime juice, and sprinkle with chopped cilantro. Garnish with cilantro sprigs, if desired.
Yield: 4 servings.

Per Serving: Calories 237 (16% from fat) Fat 4.1g (Sat 0.9g) Protein 29.1g Carbohydrate 20.2g Fiber 1.5g Cholesterol 72mg Sodium 226mg

Citrus Chicken with Roasted Corn Relish

Plain orange marmalade and regular honey mustard may be substituted for the pineapple-orange marmalade and the orange-honey mustard.

Sweet-and-Sour Chicken

Prep: 30 minutes   Cook: 45 minutes

½ cup pineapple-orange marmalade
1 tablespoon orange-honey mustard
1 tablespoon low-sodium soy sauce
½ teaspoon salt
½ teaspoon minced garlic
8 small chicken thighs (about 1½ pounds), skinned
Vegetable cooking spray
2 cups cooked long-grain rice (cooked without salt or fat)
1 teaspoon grated orange rind
Kiwifruit slices (optional)
Orange slices (optional)

1 Combine first 5 ingredients in a small saucepan. Cook over low heat until marmalade melts; remove from heat, and keep warm.

2 Place chicken in a 13- x 9- x 2-inch shallow baking dish coated with cooking spray. Bake, uncovered, at 450° for 10 minutes. Pour marmalade mixture over chicken; cover with aluminum foil and bake at 350° for 35 minutes or until chicken is done and marmalade mixture is slightly thickened.

3 Combine rice and orange rind. Spoon ½ cup rice mixture onto each serving plate. Place 2 chicken thighs over rice on each plate; spoon marmalade mixture in baking dish evenly over chicken. If desired, garnish with kiwifruit slices and orange slices.
Yield: 4 servings.

Per Serving: Calories 378 (11% from fat)   Fat 4.8g (Sat 1.1g)   Protein 24.4g   Carbohydrate 54.6g   Fiber 0.5g   Cholesterol 95mg   Sodium 544mg

Sweet-and-Sour Chicken

These chicken thighs may remind you of the spicy chicken wings served at your local sports grill. You'll need the cool blue cheese dressing to tame the heat.

Baked Buffalo Chicken

Prep: 15 minutes   Cook: 25 minutes

Vegetable cooking spray
1½ teaspoons vegetable oil
8 small chicken thighs (about 1½ pounds), skinned
¼ cup hot sauce
3 tablespoons fat-free margarine, melted
2 tablespoons water
1 tablespoon white vinegar
1 teaspoon celery seeds
⅛ teaspoon pepper
½ cup fat-free blue cheese dressing

1 Coat a nonstick skillet with cooking spray; add oil. Place over medium-high heat until hot. Add chicken; cook 4 minutes on each side. Transfer to an 11- x 7- x 1½-inch baking dish coated with cooking spray.

2 Combine hot sauce and next 5 ingredients; pour over chicken. Bake, uncovered, at 400° for 25 minutes. Serve with blue cheese dressing.
Yield: 4 servings (serving size: 2 thighs plus 2 tablespoons dressing).

Per Serving: Calories 212 (28% from fat)   Fat 6.7g (Sat 1.5g)   Protein 23.2g   Carbohydrate 11.6g   Fiber 0.7g   Cholesterol 95mg   Sodium 575mg

Cook your entire meal in only one pan with this hearty chicken and grain recipe.

Chicken and Bulgur Skillet

Prep: 5 minutes   Cook: 40 minutes

Vegetable cooking spray
1 teaspoon vegetable oil
1 (3½-pound) broiler-fryer, cut up and skinned
3 cups canned no-salt-added chicken broth
1 cup frozen chopped onion, celery, and pepper blend
¼ teaspoon salt
¼ teaspoon pepper
1½ cups bulgur (or cracked wheat), uncooked
½ teaspoon dried Italian seasoning

1 Coat a nonstick skillet with cooking spray; add oil. Place over medium-high heat until hot. Add chicken, and cook 4 minutes on each side. Add broth and next 3 ingredients to skillet. Bring to a boil; cover, reduce heat, and simmer 15 minutes. Stir in bulgur and seasoning. Cover; cook over low heat 15 minutes or until chicken is done, bulgur is tender, and liquid is absorbed.
Yield: 6 servings.

Per Serving: Calories 323 (15% from fat)   Fat 5.4g (Sat 1.2g)   Protein 32.9g   Carbohydrate 34.7g   Fiber 7.8g   Cholesterol 89mg   Sodium 212mg

Chicken Ratatouille

Prep: 19 minutes   Cook: 50 minutes

Olive oil-flavored vegetable cooking spray
1 (3-pound) broiler-fryer, cut up and skinned
2 cups sliced zucchini
2½ cups cubed eggplant
1 cup coarsely chopped onion
1 teaspoon minced garlic
1 (14½-ounce) can no-salt-added stewed tomatoes, undrained
1 tablespoon chopped fresh oregano
½ teaspoon salt
¼ teaspoon pepper

1 Coat a large nonstick skillet with cooking spray; place over medium-high heat until hot. Add chicken, and cook 3 to 5 minutes on each side or until browned. Transfer chicken to a 13- x 9- x 2-inch baking dish coated with cooking spray; set aside.

2 Coat skillet with cooking spray; place over medium-high heat until hot. Add zucchini, and sauté 3 minutes. Add eggplant, onion, and garlic; sauté 4 minutes or until vegetables are tender. Add tomato and remaining 3 ingredients; stir well.

3 Pour vegetable mixture over chicken. Cover and bake at 350° for 30 minutes. Uncover; bake 20 minutes or until chicken is done.
Yield: 6 servings.

Per Serving: Calories 170 (20% from fat)   Fat 3.7g (Sat 0.9g)   Protein 24.9g
Carbohydrate 9.0g   Fiber 0.9g   Cholesterol 76mg   Sodium 294mg

Ratatouille is a combination of eggplant, tomato, and onion cooked in olive oil. When you add chicken, it's a one-dish meal. Save yourself some time—buy a pre-cut broiler-fryer.

Loosen the skin from the chicken by running your fingers between the meat and the skin. Rub the herb mixture on the meat of the chicken, underneath the skin.

Place the lemon slices over the herb mixture.

Lemon-Herb Roasted Chicken

Prep: 10 minutes   Cook: 1 hour

1   teaspoon chopped fresh oregano
1   teaspoon chopped fresh rosemary
1   teaspoon chopped fresh thyme
½   teaspoon salt
½   teaspoon pepper
2   cloves garlic, minced
1   (3-pound) broiler-fryer
1   lemon, thinly sliced
Vegetable cooking spray
Fresh lemon slices (optional)
Fresh oregano sprigs (optional)
Fresh rosemary sprigs (optional)
Fresh thyme sprigs (optional)

1 Combine first 6 ingredients; set aside. Trim fat from chicken. Remove giblets and neck from chicken; reserve for another use. Rinse chicken under cold water, and pat dry with paper towels.

2 Carefully loosen skin from body of chicken by running fingers between skin and meat. Rub herb mixture over meat; place lemon slices over herb mixture. Lift wing tips up and over back; tuck under chicken.

3 Place chicken, breast side up, on a rack in a shallow roasting pan coated with cooking spray. Insert meat thermometer into meaty part of thigh, making sure it does not touch bone. Bake at 375° for 1 hour or until meat thermometer registers 180°. Cover loosely with aluminum foil, and let stand 15 minutes. Transfer to a serving platter. If desired, garnish with lemon slices and oregano, rosemary, and thyme sprigs. Remove and discard skin before slicing.
Yield: 6 servings.   *(Recipe pictured on page 148.)*

Per Serving: Calories 171 (35% from fat)   Fat 6.6g (Sat 1.8g)   Protein 25.7g   Carbohydrate 0.6g   Fiber 0.1g   Cholesterol 79mg   Sodium 272mg

Turkey French Bread Pizzas

Prep: 23 minutes   Cook: 5 minutes

Vegetable cooking spray
1½ pounds freshly ground raw turkey breast
1½ cups sliced fresh mushrooms
¾ cup chopped onion
1 clove garlic, crushed
1 (15-ounce) can pizza sauce
⅛ teaspoon salt
2 (8-ounce) loaves French bread
1½ cups (6 ounces) shredded part-skim mozzarella cheese

1 Coat a large nonstick skillet with cooking spray; place over medium-high heat until hot. Add turkey and next 3 ingredients. Cook until turkey is browned, stirring until it crumbles. Drain, if necessary. Stir in pizza sauce and salt; cook until thoroughly heated.

2 Cut each loaf in half horizontally; cut each horizontal piece in half crosswise. Place on an ungreased baking sheet, cut sides up. Broil 5½ inches from heat (with electric oven door partially opened) 1 minute or until lightly toasted. Spoon turkey mixture over French bread pieces; sprinkle with cheese. Broil 5½ inches from heat until cheese melts.
Yield: 8 servings.

Per Serving: Calories 355 (21% from fat)   Fat 8.4g (Sat 3.3g)   Protein 30.7g
Carbohydrate 37.6g   Fiber 3.0g   Cholesterol 56mg   Sodium 638mg

■ Why order out when you can deliver this pizza to your family in under 30 minutes?

Turkey Teriyaki

Prep: 5 minutes   Marinate: 30 minutes   Cook: 6 minutes

¼ cup low-sodium teriyaki sauce
1 tablespoon peeled, grated gingerroot
1 large clove garlic, minced
2 (½-pound) turkey tenderloins, cut into 2- x ½-inch pieces
8 large green onions, cut into 1½-inch pieces

1 Combine first 3 ingredients. Add turkey; cover and marinate in refrigerator 30 minutes. Remove turkey from marinade; reserve marinade. Place marinade in a saucepan; bring to a boil. Remove from heat.

2 Thread turkey and onion alternately onto 4 (8-inch) skewers. Broil 5½ inches from heat (with electric oven door partially opened) 3 minutes on each side or until turkey is done, basting with marinade.
Yield: 4 servings.

Per Serving: Calories 156 (16% from fat)   Fat 2.8g (Sat 0.9g)   Protein 26.5g
Carbohydrate 3.9g   Fiber 0.2g   Cholesterol 59mg   Sodium 356mg

You can also spoon this casserole mixture into a 1½-quart baking dish coated with cooking spray. Top with potatoes, and bake at 400° for 25 to 30 minutes or until potatoes are lightly browned.

Turkey-Potato Casserole

Prep: 15 minutes   Bake: 15 minutes

¾ pound ground turkey sausage
1 (10¾-ounce) can reduced-fat, reduced-sodium cream of chicken soup
2½ cups 1% low-fat milk, divided
1 tablespoon all-purpose flour
1 (10-ounce) package frozen peas and carrots, thawed
Vegetable cooking spray
3 cups frozen mashed potatoes
Paprika (optional)
Chopped fresh parsley (optional)

1 Cook turkey sausage in a nonstick skillet over medium-high heat until browned, stirring until it crumbles. Drain, if necessary. Add soup; stir well.

2 Combine 1 cup milk and flour, stirring until smooth. Add milk mixture to turkey mixture; bring to a boil. Stir in peas and carrots. Reduce heat, and cook, uncovered, 2 to 3 minutes or until turkey mixture is slightly thickened, stirring occasionally. Place 1 cup mixture into each of 6 (8-ounce) ovenproof casserole dishes coated with cooking spray.

3 Prepare potatoes according to package directions, using remaining 1½ cups milk. Top each casserole with ½ cup mashed potato mixture. Sprinkle with paprika, if desired. Bake at 400° for 15 to 20 minutes or until turkey mixture is thoroughly heated and potatoes are lightly browned. Sprinkle with chopped parsley, if desired.
Yield: 6 servings.

Per Serving: Calories 267 (34% from fat)   Fat 10.0g (Sat 4.2g)   Protein 15.9g
Carbohydrate 24.4g   Fiber 2.5g   Cholesterol 46mg   Sodium 687mg

Turkey Tenderloins with Black Bean Salsa

Prep: 12 minutes   Marinate: 20 minutes   Cook: 16 minutes

1 (15-ounce) can no-salt-added black beans, drained
1 cup no-salt-added salsa
½ cup fresh lime juice
½ teaspoon ground red pepper
½ teaspoon ground cumin
¼ teaspoon salt
4 cloves garlic, crushed
2 (½-pound) turkey tenderloins
Vegetable cooking spray

1 Combine black beans and salsa, stirring well. Cover and chill.

2 Combine lime juice and next 4 ingredients in a heavy-duty, zip-top plastic bag. Add turkey; seal bag, and shake until turkey is well coated. Marinate in refrigerator 20 minutes, turning bag once.

3 Remove turkey from marinade, reserving marinade. Place marinade in a small saucepan; bring to a boil. Remove from heat, and set aside. Coat grill rack with cooking spray; place on grill over medium-hot coals (350° to 400°). Place turkey on rack; grill, covered, 8 to 10 minutes on each side or until turkey is done, turning and basting with reserved marinade. Cut turkey diagonally across grain into thin slices. Serve with Black Bean Salsa.
Yield: 4 servings.

Per Serving: Calories 264 (12% from fat)   Fat 3.6g (Sat 1.0g)   Protein 33.2g   Carbohydrate 24.5g   Fiber 3.2g   Cholesterol 59mg   Sodium 284mg

■ This dish pairs a black bean salsa with grilled turkey, but you may want to serve the salsa with baked tortilla chips for a quick appetizer.

Salads

People often say, "I'll just have a salad," like a salad is second-class food. When I create a salad, it's first class all the way—a bowl brimming with crisp greens, juicy tomatoes, crunchy croutons, and creamy dressing.

My salads are fresh, flavorful, filling, and so easy to throw together. Short of a visit to the "all-you-care-to-eat" salad bar, a simple salad may be the quickest way to dinner.

Cornbread Salad (page 171)

169

Autumn Fruit Salad

Prep: 20 minutes

1 (8-ounce) carton low-fat sour cream
¼ cup firmly packed brown sugar
½ teaspoon ground cinnamon
1¾ cups sliced banana
1½ cups chopped apple
1½ cups chopped pear
1¼ cups fresh orange sections

1 Combine first 3 ingredients, stirring well. Combine banana and remaining 3 ingredients in a large bowl; toss well. To serve, spoon sour cream mixture evenly over fruit.
Yield: 7 (1-cup) servings.

Per Serving: Calories 171 (23% from fat)   Fat 4.4g (Sat 2.5g)   Protein 2.0g   Carbohydrate 34.0g   Fiber 4.9g   Cholesterol 12mg   Sodium 16mg

The sweet, creamy dressing on this salad enhances the flavor of any fruit. In the summer, spoon the topping over fresh melon, berries, or peaches.

Melon-Cucumber Salad

Prep: 10 minutes   Chill: 1 hour

1 medium cucumber
3 cups cubed cantaloupe
2 tablespoons limeade concentrate, undiluted
1 tablespoon water
1 teaspoon vegetable oil
½ teaspoon chili powder

1 Cut cucumber in half lengthwise; cut each half crosswise into ¼-inch-thick slices. Combine cucumber and cantaloupe in a medium bowl.

2 Combine limeade concentrate and remaining 3 ingredients, stirring well. Pour limeade mixture over cantaloupe mixture; toss lightly. Cover and chill thoroughly. Toss lightly before serving.
Yield: 4 (1-cup) servings.   *(Salad pictured on page 16.)*

Per Serving: Calories 64 (20% from fat)   Fat 1.4g (Sat 0.3g)   Protein 0.8g   Carbohydrate 13.6g   Fiber 1.6g   Cholesterol 0mg   Sodium 12mg

This sweet and tangy salad is just as delicious with honeydew melon.

Arugula with Sun-Dried Tomatoes

Prep: 10 minutes   Stand: 10 minutes

8 sun-dried tomatoes (packed without oil)
½ cup hot water
⅓ cup fat-free French dressing
1 tablespoon balsamic vinegar
1 tablespoon unsweetened apple juice
1 teaspoon Dijon mustard
⅛ teaspoon pepper
4 cups torn arugula
¼ cup freshly grated Parmesan cheese

1 Combine tomatoes and hot water in a small bowl; let stand 10 minutes. Drain and cut tomatoes into quarters.

2 Combine dressing and next 4 ingredients in a small bowl, stirring well. Combine tomato and arugula in a bowl, tossing lightly. Drizzle dressing mixture over arugula mixture. Sprinkle with Parmesan cheese.
Yield: 4 (1-cup) servings.

Per Serving: Calories 69 (29% from fat)   Fat 2.2g (Sat 1.2g)   Protein 3.6g
Carbohydrate 8.9g   Fiber 1.4g   Cholesterol 5mg   Sodium 317mg

■ Arugula is a salad green that looks similar to radish leaves or dandelion greens. Its dark green leaves have a pungent peppery flavor. If you can't find arugula, use torn fresh spinach.

Cornbread Salad

Prep: 35 minutes

1 (7.5-ounce) package corn muffin mix
6 cups torn romaine lettuce
1 cup seeded, chopped tomato
1 cup chopped green pepper
¾ cup chopped purple onion
3 slices turkey bacon, cooked and crumbled
⅔ cup fat-free Ranch-style dressing

1 Prepare muffin mix according to package directions in an 8-inch square pan, using water instead of milk. Cool 10 minutes. Remove cornbread from pan; cut into cubes. Place cornbread cubes on a baking sheet; bake at 400° for 10 minutes or until crisp and lightly browned. Place half of cornbread cubes in a large bowl; reserve remaining cornbread cubes for another use.

2 Combine cornbread cubes, lettuce, and next 4 ingredients; toss well. Pour dressing over salad, and toss well. Serve immediately.
Yield: 6 (2-cup) servings.   *(Recipe pictured on page 168.)*

Per Serving: Calories 152 (15% from fat)   Fat 2.6g (Sat 0.5g)   Protein 4.1g
Carbohydrate 27.7g   Fiber 1.8g   Cholesterol 5mg   Sodium 501mg

■ Prepare the rest of the ingredients while the cornbread bakes. Or, make the cornbread cubes a few days early, and store them in an airtight container up to three days.

Turn a Tomato into a Cup

Cut about ½ inch off the top of each tomato. For a decorative touch, cut a scalloped edge on the top of each cup using a sharp knife.

Scoop out the pulp to make a shell.

Invert the tomato cups on paper towels to drain.

Vegetable-Rice Salad in Tomato Cups

Prep: 20 minutes   Stand/Chill: 30 minutes

6 large tomatoes
3 cups cooked long-grain rice (cooked without salt or fat)
1 (15-ounce) can no-salt-added black beans, drained
1 (10-ounce) package frozen whole-kernel corn, thawed
½ cup chopped purple onion
½ cup reduced-fat olive oil vinaigrette
1 tablespoon chopped fresh cilantro
Fresh cilantro sprig (optional)

1 Cut top off each tomato. Scoop out pulp, leaving ¼-inch-thick shells. Chop pulp to measure 1 cup; reserve remaining pulp for another use. Invert tomato shells on paper towels, and let stand 30 minutes.

2 While tomato shells stand, combine 1 cup chopped tomato pulp, rice, and next 5 ingredients in a medium bowl. Cover and chill 30 minutes.

3 To serve, spoon rice mixture evenly into tomato shells. Garnish with fresh cilantro, if desired.
Yield: 6 servings.

Per Serving: Calories 290 (16% from fat)   Fat 5.3g (Sat 0.5g)   Protein 9.0g
Carbohydrate 55.7g   Fiber 6.1g   Cholesterol 0mg   Sodium 179mg

Vegetable-Rice Salad in Tomato Cups

Black-Eyed Pea and Rice Salad

Prep: 10 minutes Cook: 25 minutes

3 cups water
½ cup chopped onion
½ cup chopped celery
¼ teaspoon salt
¼ teaspoon pepper
4 ounces Canadian bacon, coarsely chopped
2 (15-ounce) cans black-eyed peas, drained
1 (10-ounce) package frozen turnip greens, thawed
1½ cups long-grain rice, uncooked
1 tablespoon drained, minced hot peppers in vinegar

1 Combine first 8 ingredients in a large saucepan. Bring to a boil; stir in rice. Cover, reduce heat, and simmer 25 minutes or until rice is tender and liquid is absorbed. Add minced hot peppers; toss well. Serve warm or chilled.
Yield: 8 (1-cup) servings.

Per Serving: Calories 233 (7% from fat) Fat 1.9g (Sat 0.5g) Protein 11.3g Carbohydrate 42.7g Fiber 2.6g Cholesterol 7mg Sodium 465mg

---

■ Use regular long-grain rice in this salad instead of instant. If you use instant, you'll end up with too much liquid in the saucepan.

White Bean and Tomato Salad

Prep: 15 minutes Stand: 30 minutes

2 (15-ounce) cans cannellini beans (or Great Northern Beans), drained
1½ cups chopped tomato
⅓ cup shredded fresh basil
⅓ cup crumbled feta cheese
¼ cup white balsamic vinegar
1½ tablespoons olive oil
½ teaspoon sugar
¼ teaspoon salt
¼ teaspoon freshly ground pepper
Green leaf lettuce leaves (optional)

1 Combine first 4 ingredients in a bowl; set aside.

2 Combine vinegar and next 4 ingredients in a small jar. Cover tightly, and shake vigorously. Pour vinegar mixture over bean mixture. Let stand at room temperature 30 minutes, stirring occasionally. Serve on lettuce-lined salad plates, if desired.
Yield: 6 (¾-cup) servings.

Per Serving: Calories 142 (35% from fat) Fat 5.6g (Sat 1.7g) Protein 6.1g Carbohydrate 16.4g Fiber 2.8g Cholesterol 7mg Sodium 512mg

---

■ Either regular or white balsamic vinegar will give this salad a great flavor, but the white balsamic won't make the beans look dark.

Succotash Slaw

Prep: 20 minutes

1 cup frozen baby lima beans
2 cups shredded cabbage
1 cup frozen whole-kernel corn, thawed
½ cup chopped sweet red pepper
¼ cup sliced green onions
¼ cup fat-free Ranch-style dressing
2 tablespoons nonfat sour cream

1 Cook lima beans according to package directions, omitting salt. Drain; rinse with cold water, and drain again.

2 Combine lima beans, cabbage, and next 3 ingredients in a large bowl. Combine dressing and sour cream. Pour dressing mixture over cabbage mixture; toss well.
Yield: 5 (¾-cup) servings.

Per Serving: Calories 100 (4% from fat)   Fat 0.4g (Sat 0.1g)   Protein 4.7g
Carbohydrate 20.5g   Fiber 2.3g   Cholesterol 0mg   Sodium 185mg

■ "Succotash" comes from a Native American word for boiled corn. In the southern part of the United States, it's a popular side dish made from lima beans, corn, and red or green peppers.

Blue Cheese-Green Bean Potato Salad

Prep: 20 minutes

1 pound small round red potatoes
1 (10-ounce) package frozen cut green beans
⅓ cup red wine vinegar
2 teaspoons vegetable oil
2 teaspoons sugar
¼ teaspoon salt
⅛ teaspoon pepper
¼ cup crumbled blue cheese
2 slices turkey bacon, cooked and crumbled

1 Cut each potato into 8 pieces. Cook potato in boiling water to cover 10 minutes. Add beans, and cook 5 additional minutes or until potato is tender. Drain well, and place in a large bowl.

2 Combine vinegar and next 4 ingredients in a small bowl, stirring well. Pour vinegar mixture over potato mixture; toss lightly. Top with blue cheese and bacon.
Yield: 6 (¾-cup) servings.

Per Serving: Calories 117 (28% from fat)   Fat 3.7g (Sat 1.4g)   Protein 4.2g
Carbohydrate 17.6g   Fiber 2.7g   Cholesterol 7mg   Sodium 242mg

■ Dish up this cheesy potato salad right away, or refrigerate and serve it the next day as a chilled salad.

Pesto Potato Salad

Pesto Potato Salad

Prep: 35 minutes

½ cup dried tomatoes (packed without oil)
½ cup hot water
2 pounds small round red potatoes
Olive oil-flavored vegetable cooking spray
½ cup sliced green onions
2 cloves garlic, minced
⅓ cup reduced-fat Caesar dressing
½ cup nonfat sour cream
2 tablespoons pesto
¼ teaspoon freshly ground pepper

1 Coarsely chop tomatoes. Combine tomato and hot water in a small bowl; let stand 10 minutes. Drain and set aside.

2 Cut potatoes into 1-inch pieces. Cook potato in boiling water to cover 15 to 17 minutes or until tender. Let cool slightly.

3 Coat a large nonstick skillet with cooking spray; place over medium-high heat until hot. Add tomato, potato, green onions, and garlic to skillet; sauté 5 minutes. Add dressing, deglazing skillet by scraping particles that cling to bottom. Cook 1 minute; set aside, and keep warm.

4 Combine sour cream, pesto, and pepper in a large bowl, stirring well. Add potato mixture, and toss lightly until combined.
Yield: 6 (1-cup) servings.

Per Serving: Calories 201 (26% from fat)   Fat 5.7g (Sat 0.8g)   Protein 6.1g
Carbohydrate 32.0g   Fiber 3.8g   Cholesterol 3mg   Sodium 446mg

Shear Force

The easiest way to cut up dried tomatoes is to use your kitchen shears.

You'll get the best flavor when you roast the potatoes, but if you're in a hurry, boil them, and add the vinaigrette, rosemary, and pepper to the dressing mixture.

Roasted Potato and Red Pepper Salad

Prep: 15 minutes   **Stand:** 15 minutes   **Cook:** 40 minutes

1½ pounds small round red potatoes
1 tablespoon minced fresh rosemary
¼ teaspoon freshly ground pepper
¼ cup reduced-fat olive oil vinaigrette, divided
Olive oil-flavored vegetable cooking spray
⅓ cup reduced-fat mayonnaise
2 tablespoons freshly grated Asiago (or Parmesan) cheese
1 (12-ounce) jar roasted red peppers, drained, rinsed, and cut into
        1-inch pieces

1 Cut potatoes into 1-inch pieces. Combine potato, rosemary, and ¼ teaspoon pepper in a large bowl. Add 2 tablespoons vinaigrette; toss well. Let stand 15 minutes.

2 Place potato mixture in a shallow roasting pan coated with cooking spray. Bake at 400° for 40 to 45 minutes or until potato is tender. Let cool slightly.

3 Combine remaining 2 tablespoons vinaigrette, mayonnaise, and cheese in a large bowl, stirring well. Add roasted potato mixture and roasted pepper; toss lightly.
Yield: 6 (¾-cup) servings.

Per Serving: Calories 156 (22% from fat)   Fat 3.8g (Sat 0.6g)   Protein 3.4g
Carbohydrate 27.8g   Fiber 2.1g   Cholesterol 2mg   Sodium 320mg

Pasta-Vegetable Salad

Prep: 15 minutes   Chill: 1 hour

6 ounces tricolor fusilli (corkscrew pasta), uncooked
1 (16-ounce) package frozen broccoli, onion, red pepper, and
     mushrooms, thawed
1 (11-ounce) package frozen asparagus spears, thawed and cut into
     1-inch pieces
1 (9-ounce) package frozen artichoke hearts, thawed
½ cup tomato chutney
½ cup reduced-fat Pesto-Parmesan salad dressing (such as Maple
     Grove Farms Lite Pesto-Parmesan dressing)
½ teaspoon freshly ground pepper
½ cup freshly grated Parmesan cheese

1 Cook pasta according to package directions, omitting salt and fat.
Drain; rinse with cold water, and drain again. Place pasta in a large
bowl; set aside.

2 Drain thawed vegetables, and press lightly between paper towels
to remove excess moisture. Add vegetables, chutney, dressing, and
pepper to pasta; toss lightly. Cover and chill thoroughly. Sprinkle
with cheese just before serving.
Yield: 7 (1-cup) servings.

Per Serving: Calories 234 (21% from fat)   Fat 5.4g (Sat 1.8g)   Protein 9.1g
Carbohydrate 38.6g   Fiber 2.7g   Cholesterol 4mg   Sodium 338mg

■ Create your own variations
of this salad by using other
frozen vegetable combinations
in similar package sizes.

Gingered Tenderloin Salad

Gingered Tenderloin Salad

Prep: 15 minutes   Marinate: 2 hours   Cook: 20 minutes

½ cup ginger preserves
⅓ cup rice vinegar
⅓ cup low-sodium soy sauce
1½ tablespoons dark sesame oil
1 (1-pound) pork tenderloin
Vegetable cooking spray
6 cups shredded napa cabbage (or other Chinese cabbage)
1 cup thinly sliced sweet red pepper

1 Combine first 4 ingredients in a small saucepan. Place over medium heat; bring to a boil, stirring constantly. Remove from heat, and let cool completely.

2 Trim fat from tenderloin. Place tenderloin in a large heavy-duty, zip-top plastic bag. Pour half of soy sauce mixture over tenderloin; reserve remaining soy sauce mixture. Seal bag, and shake until tenderloin is well coated. Marinate in refrigerator at least 2 hours, turning bag occasionally.

3 Remove tenderloin from marinade, reserving marinade. Insert meat thermometer into thickest part of tenderloin, if desired. Place marinade in a small saucepan. Bring to a boil; remove from heat, and set aside. Coat grill rack with cooking spray; place on grill over medium-hot coals (350° to 400°). Place tenderloin on rack; grill, covered, 20 minutes or until meat thermometer registers 160°, turning and basting occasionally with reserved marinade. Let tenderloin stand 10 minutes; slice diagonally across grain into thin slices.

4 Combine cabbage and red pepper. Pour remaining half of soy sauce mixture over cabbage mixture; toss lightly. Spoon cabbage mixture evenly onto individual salad plates. Arrange tenderloin slices over cabbage mixture.
Yield: 4 servings.

Per Serving: Calories 252 (22% from fat)   Fat 6.1g (Sat 1.7g)   Protein 25.8g
Carbohydrate 24.0g   Fiber 0.9g   Cholesterol 79mg   Sodium 269mg

■ You only have to marinate the tenderloin for two hours in this sweet, tangy marinade to capture the distinct Asian flavor combination of ginger, soy, and sesame. (If ginger preserves are not available, combine ½ cup low-sugar orange marmalade and 1½ tablespoons minced fresh gingerroot.)

Toast the leftover French bread to make extra croutons for salads. Store croutons in a zip-top plastic bag.

Grilled Chicken Caesar Salad

Prep: 14 minutes   Marinate: 1 hour   Cook: 10 minutes

4 (4-ounce) skinned, boned chicken breast halves
½ cup reduced-fat Caesar dressing, divided
2 cups cubed French bread
Olive oil-flavored vegetable cooking spray
6 cups torn romaine lettuce
1 cup sliced cucumber
2 medium tomatoes, each cut into 8 wedges
2 tablespoons freshly grated Parmesan cheese
Freshly ground pepper (optional)

1 Place chicken in a heavy-duty, zip-top plastic bag; pour ¼ cup dressing over chicken. Seal bag, and shake until chicken is well coated. Marinate in refrigerator 1 hour, turning bag once.

2 Coat French bread cubes with cooking spray; place in a single layer on a baking sheet. Bake at 350° for 10 minutes or until lightly browned.

3 Remove chicken from marinade, discarding marinade. Coat grill rack with cooking spray; place on grill over medium-hot coals (350° to 400°). Place chicken on rack; grill, covered, 5 minutes on each side or until done. Let cool slightly. Cut chicken crosswise into ¼-inch-thick slices.

4 Combine chicken, bread cubes, lettuce, and next 3 ingredients in a large serving bowl. Pour remaining ¼ cup dressing over lettuce mixture, and toss well. Sprinkle with freshly ground pepper, if desired. Serve immediately.
Yield: 6 (2-cup) servings.

Per Serving: Calories 206 (31% from fat)   Fat 7.2g (Sat 1.3g)   Protein 20.5g
Carbohydrate 13.0g   Fiber 1.7g   Cholesterol 53mg   Sodium 554mg

Grilled Chicken Caesar Salad

Look for mango chutney near the relishes, pickles, and other condiments in the grocery store.

Peachy Chicken Salad

Prep: 8 minutes   Cook: 15 minutes   Chill: 1 hour

1 cup chopped frozen peaches, slightly thawed
2 tablespoons peeled, minced gingerroot
2 tablespoons low-sodium soy sauce
1 (9-ounce) jar mango chutney
4 cups chopped cooked chicken breast (skinned before cooking and cooked without salt)
1 cup chopped sweet red pepper
1 (8-ounce) can chopped water chestnuts, drained
6 Boston lettuce leaves (optional)

1 Combine first 4 ingredients in a small saucepan. Bring to a boil. Reduce heat, and simmer, uncovered, 10 to 15 minutes or until thickened, stirring often. Let cool.

2 Combine cooled chutney mixture, chicken, red pepper, and water chestnuts in a large bowl, stirring well. Cover and chill thoroughly. Serve on lettuce-lined salad plates, if desired.
Yield: 6 (1-cup) servings.

Per Serving: Calories 332 (9% from fat)   Fat 3.5g (Sat 1.0g)   Protein 30.1g Carbohydrate 40.6g   Fiber 1.0g   Cholesterol 80mg   Sodium 573mg

If papayas aren't available, substitute fresh cantaloupe wedges.

Crab-Papaya Salad

Prep: 20 minutes   Chill: 1 hour

½ cup chopped sweet red pepper
⅓ cup reduced-fat mayonnaise
¼ cup chopped green onions
¼ cup mango chutney
1½ tablespoons horseradish mustard
¼ teaspoon freshly ground pepper
1 pound fresh lump crabmeat, drained
3 small papayas, peeled, cut in half lengthwise, and seeded
Green leaf lettuce leaves (optional)

1 Combine first 7 ingredients in a small bowl, stirring well. Cover and chill.

2 To serve, spoon ½ cup crab mixture into each papaya half. Place papaya halves on individual lettuce-lined salad plates, if desired.
Yield: 6 servings.

Per Serving: Calories 202 (23% from fat)   Fat 5.2g (Sat 0.8g)   Protein 15.3g Carbohydrate 23.2g   Fiber 2.4g   Cholesterol 75mg   Sodium 478mg

Grilled Salmon Salad

Prep: 15 minutes   Marinate: 8 hours   Cook: 8 minutes

½ cup plus 1 tablespoon molasses, divided
¼ cup plus 1 tablespoon peppercorn mustard, divided
¼ cup plus 1 tablespoon malt vinegar, divided
6 (4-ounce) salmon fillets
2 large purple onions, sliced
Vegetable cooking spray
8 cups mixed baby salad greens
2 teaspoons vegetable oil
⅛ teaspoon salt

1 Combine ½ cup molasses, ¼ cup mustard, and 3 tablespoons vinegar, stirring well. Place salmon and onion in a shallow dish. Pour molasses mixture over salmon and onion. Cover and marinate in refrigerator 8 hours, turning occasionally.

2 Remove salmon and onion from marinade, reserving marinade. Place marinade in a small saucepan. Bring to a boil; cook 1 minute. Coat grill rack with cooking spray; place on grill over medium-hot coals (350° to 400°). Place salmon and onion on rack; grill, covered, 4 minutes on each side, or until fish flakes easily when tested with a fork and onion is tender, basting often with reserved marinade.

3 Combine onion and greens. Combine remaining 1 tablespoon molasses, 1 tablespoon mustard, 2 tablespoons vinegar, oil, and salt. Pour molasses mixture over greens mixture; toss lightly. Spoon evenly onto individual serving plates. Top each serving with a fillet.
Yield: 6 servings.

Per Serving: Calories 327 (33% from fat)   Fat 12.0g (Sat 1.9g)   Protein 24.4g
Carbohydrate 29.2g   Fiber 1.6g   Cholesterol 74mg   Sodium 495mg

■ Make your own peppercorn mustard with ½ teaspoon cracked pepper and ¼ cup plus 1 tablespoon Dijon mustard.

Watercress adds a slightly bitter, peppery flavor to the salad, but if watercress isn't available, use romaine or curly-leaf lettuce.

Scallop and Watercress Salad

Prep: 20 minutes

Vegetable cooking spray
1 pound sea scallops
1 cup sweet red pepper strips
2 cloves garlic, minced
¼ cup plus 2 tablespoons reduced-fat olive oil vinaigrette
1 tablespoon lemon juice
5 cups torn Bibb lettuce
1 cup tightly packed watercress leaves
½ teaspoon freshly ground pepper

1 Coat a large cast-iron skillet with cooking spray; place over high heat until hot. Add scallops; cook 2 minutes on each side or until browned. Remove scallops from skillet; set aside, and keep warm.

2 Coat skillet with cooking spray. Place over medium-high heat until hot. Add pepper strips and garlic; sauté 2 minutes or until tender. Add vinaigrette and lemon juice, deglazing skillet by scraping particles that cling to bottom. Cook 1 minute. Return scallops to skillet, and cook until thoroughly heated.

3 Combine lettuce and watercress in a large bowl. Add scallop mixture to lettuce mixture; toss lightly. Sprinkle with ½ teaspoon pepper. **Yield: 4 (1¼-cup) servings.**

Per Serving: Calories 165 (32% from fat)   Fat 5.9g (Sat 0.5g)   Protein 20.0g
Carbohydrate 8.5g   Fiber 1.0g   Cholesterol 37mg   Sodium 369mg

Thai Shrimp and Pasta Salad

Prep: 30 minutes

6 ounces farfalle (bow tie pasta), uncooked
1 pound unpeeled medium-size fresh shrimp
2 teaspoons hot chile oil
2 teaspoons commercial roasted minced garlic
½ cup low-fat spicy Indonesian dressing
1 cup green pepper strips
¼ teaspoon freshly ground pepper
1 (15-ounce) can straw mushrooms, drained
Lime wedges (optional)

1 Cook pasta according to package directions, omitting salt and fat. Drain; rinse with cold water, and drain again. Place pasta in a large bowl; set aside.

2 Peel and devein shrimp. Heat oil in a large nonstick skillet over medium-high heat until hot. Add shrimp and garlic; sauté 3 minutes or until shrimp turn pink. Add dressing to skillet, deglazing skillet by scraping particles that cling to bottom. Stir in green pepper, ground pepper, and mushrooms. Bring to a boil; reduce heat, and simmer, uncovered, 2 minutes.

3 Add shrimp mixture to pasta; toss lightly. Serve warm or chilled. Garnish with lime wedges, if desired.
Yield: 4 (1½-cup) servings.

Per Serving: Calories 322 (20% from fat)   Fat 7.2g (Sat 1.3g)   Protein 25.0g
Carbohydrate 39.6g   Fiber 1.3g   Cholesterol 129mg   Sodium 533mg

■ The Indonesian dressing (with its touch of peanut butter, soy sauce, and red pepper) is what makes this salad wonderful. If your grocery store doesn't have it, use a reduced-fat sweet-and-sour dressing.

Thai Shrimp and Pasta Salad

Sandwiches ... Snacks

I think the Earl of Sandwich had the right idea. Get a slice of bread, add some meat, cheese, and vegetables, top them with another slice of bread, and you have a meal. What could be easier?

And, if you eat a sandwich for supper as often as I do, you can vary your menu simply by putting your sandwich filling on another type of bread, changing the cheese, or adding a flavored mustard. Just because sandwiches are easy doesn't mean they have to be boring.

Club Sandwich (page 200)

■ Breakfast is a snap with these simple sandwiches. Buy peeled and cored pineapple to keep prep time to 10 minutes.

Breakfast Bagel Stack-Ups

Prep: 10 minutes

½ (8-ounce) package light process cream cheese, softened
1 tablespoon brown sugar
4 plain bagels, split
¼ cup sliced fresh strawberries
4 (¼-inch-thick) slices fresh pineapple

1 Combine cream cheese and sugar in a small bowl, stirring well. Spread cheese mixture evenly over cut sides of 4 bagel halves. Place strawberry slices evenly over cheese mixture; top each serving with a pineapple slice. Top with remaining bagel halves.
Yield: 4 servings.

Per Serving: Calories 388 (16% from fat) Fat 7.0g (Sat 2.9g) Protein 14.2g Carbohydrate 70.0g Fiber 4.0g Cholesterol 16mg Sodium 612mg

■ ■ ■

Blueberry Bagel Stack-Ups: Substitute ¼ cup fresh blueberries for the strawberries, and use blueberry bagels instead of plain.

Per Serving: Calories 390 (16% from fat) Fat 7.0g (Sat 2.9g) Protein 14.2g Carbohydrate 70.6g Fiber 4.2g Cholesterol 16mg Sodium 612mg

■ Fat-free Cheddar gives this sandwich a sharp cheese flavor, but any combination of fat-free cheeses will work.

Glorified Grilled Cheese

Prep: 15 minutes   Cook: 3 minutes

⅓ cup Neufchâtel cheese, softened
½ teaspoon dried basil
8 (1-ounce) slices white or whole wheat bread
4 (¾-ounce) slices fat-free sharp Cheddar cheese
4 (¾-ounce) slices fat-free mozzarella cheese
1 tablespoon plus 1 teaspoon reduced-calorie margarine, softened
Vegetable cooking spray

1 Combine Neufchâtel cheese and basil, stirring well. Spread cheese mixture evenly over one side of 4 bread slices. Place cheese slices over cheese mixture; top with remaining bread slices.

2 Spread margarine evenly over both sides of sandwiches. Place in a sandwich press or hot skillet coated with cooking spray. Cook until bread is lightly browned and cheese melts. Serve immediately.
Yield: 4 servings. *(Sandwich pictured on page 12.)*

Per Serving: Calories 283 (27% from fat) Fat 8.4g (Sat 3.4g) Protein 17.7g Carbohydrate 33.7g Fiber 1.1g Cholesterol 22mg Sodium 898mg

Breakfast Bagel Stack-Ups

■ Grilled eggplant slices instead of bread hold the cheesy vegetable mixture for these knife-and-fork sandwiches.

Slice It

Cut 2 (½-inch-thick) slices from the opposite lengthwise sides of the eggplant. (These slices have a rounded skin edge and won't work well for the sandwich.)

Slice the remaining eggplant into 4 lengthwise slices with flesh on both sides.

Grilled Eggplant Sandwiches

Prep: 10 minutes   Cook: 18 minutes

2 medium eggplants (about 2 pounds)
2 medium-size sweet red peppers
2 small zucchini
Vegetable cooking spray
⅓ cup fat-free Italian dressing
¼ cup drained, sliced pepperoncini peppers
4 (1-ounce) slices part-skim mozzarella cheese

1 Cut 2 (½-inch-thick) slices lengthwise from opposite sides of each eggplant; reserve for another use. Cut each eggplant lengthwise into 4 (¾-inch-thick) slices; set aside.

2 Cut red peppers in half lengthwise; remove and discard seeds and membranes. Flatten pepper halves with palm of hand; set aside. Cut zucchini lengthwise into ¼-inch-thick slices.

3 Coat grill rack with cooking spray; place on grill over medium-hot coals (350° to 400°). Brush eggplant, red pepper, and zucchini with about one-third of dressing. Place red pepper and zucchini on rack; grill, covered, 6 minutes. Turn vegetables, and baste with half of remaining dressing. Add eggplant to grill rack; grill, covered, 10 minutes, turning once, and basting often with remaining dressing.

4 Arrange pepper halves and zucchini slices evenly over 4 eggplant slices; sprinkle with pepperoncini pepper. Place 1 slice of cheese over each serving. Top with remaining eggplant slices. Grill 2 additional minutes or until cheese melts. Serve immediately.
Yield: 4 servings.

Per Serving: Calories 170 (29% from fat)   Fat 5.4g (Sat 3.0g)   Protein 10.8g   Carbohydrate 23.0g   Fiber 5.0g   Cholesterol 16mg   Sodium 438mg

Antipasto Sandwiches

Prep: 15 minutes

2 (6-ounce) cans low-sodium white tuna packed in water, drained
¼ cup fat-free zesty Italian dressing
1 (12-ounce) loaf Italian bread, split horizontally and toasted
4 romaine lettuce leaves
2 plum tomatoes, sliced
3 (2-ounce) slices part-skim mozzarella cheese
2 tablespoons chopped ripe olives

1 Combine tuna and dressing; toss well. Spoon tuna mixture over bottom half of bread. Arrange lettuce, sliced tomato, and cheese evenly over tuna mixture; sprinkle with olives. Top with remaining bread half. Cut into 6 pieces.
Yield: 6 servings.

Per Serving: Calories 294 (18% from fat) Fat 6.0g (Sat 3.1g) Protein 24.1g
Carbohydrate 56.1g Fiber 2.0g Cholesterol 38mg Sodium 644mg

■ Antipasto is an Italian term for an appetizer assortment of meats, olives, cheeses, and marinated vegetables. Here, the appetizer ingredients are stacked on toasted Italian bread.

Shrimp Louis Boats

Prep: 20 minutes   Chill: 15 minutes

3 (2½-ounce) submarine rolls, split
1½ pounds unpeeled medium-size fresh shrimp
1½ quarts water
½ cup nonfat mayonnaise
2 tablespoons chopped green onions
1 tablespoon chili sauce
¾ teaspoon salt-free lemon pepper
12 Bibb lettuce leaves

1 Hollow out centers of rolls, leaving ½-inch-thick shells. Reserve insides of rolls for another use.

2 Peel and devein shrimp. Bring water to a boil; add shrimp, and cook 3 to 5 minutes or until shrimp turn pink. Drain well; rinse with cold water. Cover and chill at least 15 minutes.

3 Combine mayonnaise and next 3 ingredients, stirring well. Stir in shrimp. Line each roll half with 2 lettuce leaves. Spoon shrimp mixture evenly over lettuce.
Yield: 6 servings.

Per Serving: Calories 184 (13% from fat) Fat 2.6g (Sat 0.6g) Protein 16.8g
Carbohydrate 22.4g Fiber 0.3g Cholesterol 124mg Sodium 644mg

■ This creamy sandwich filling is also delicious as a luncheon salad. Spoon it over crisp lettuce, and serve with fat-free crackers.

Crab Cake Sandwich

Crab Cake Sandwiches

Prep: 20 minutes   Chill: 30 minutes   Cook: 8 minutes

1 (2-ounce) jar diced pimiento
¼ cup plus 2 tablespoons low-fat mayonnaise
¾ pound fresh lump crabmeat, drained
⅔ cup fine, dry breadcrumbs, divided
¼ teaspoon pepper
1 egg white
Vegetable cooking spray
4 green leaf lettuce leaves
4 reduced-calorie whole wheat hamburger buns

1 Drain pimiento, and press between paper towels to remove excess moisture. Combine pimiento and mayonnaise, stirring well. Combine 2 tablespoons pimiento mixture, crabmeat, ⅓ cup breadcrumbs, pepper, and egg white in a bowl; stir lightly. Set remaining pimiento mixture aside.

2 Shape crabmeat mixture into 4 (¾-inch-thick) patties. Dredge patties in remaining ⅓ cup breadcrumbs. Place patties on a baking sheet; cover and chill 30 minutes.

3 Coat a large nonstick skillet with cooking spray; place over medium heat until hot. Add patties, and cook 4 minutes on each side or until lightly browned.

4 Place 1 lettuce leaf on bottom half of each bun; top with crab cakes. Spread remaining pimiento mixture evenly over crab cakes. Top with remaining bun halves. Serve immediately.
Yield: 4 servings.

Per Serving: Calories 260 (15% from fat)   Fat 4.2g (Sat 0.4g)   Protein 21.3g
Carbohydrate 38.3g   Fiber 5.8g   Cholesterol 71mg   Sodium 790mg

■ Fresh crabmeat usually comes in 1-pound containers, so you'll have about ¼ pound extra for another use.

Don't buy split rolls for this sandwich. You'll need whole rolls to make large enough bread shells to hold the filling.

Curried Onion and Beef Subs

Prep: 40 minutes

Vegetable cooking spray
3 medium onions, thinly sliced
1½ teaspoons curry powder
1 teaspoon commercial roasted minced garlic
4 (2½-ounce) whole wheat submarine rolls
2 tablespoons nonfat mayonnaise
2 tablespoons coarse-grained mustard
½ pound thinly sliced lean roast beef

1 Coat a large nonstick skillet with cooking spray; place over medium-high heat until hot. Add onion; sauté 5 minutes. Reduce heat to medium-low; cook 20 to 25 minutes or until onion is golden. Stir in curry powder and garlic; cook, stirring constantly, 5 additional minutes.

2 Cut a ½-inch-thick slice off top of each roll; set tops aside. Hollow out centers of rolls, leaving ½-inch-thick shells. Reserve insides of rolls for another use.

3 Combine mayonnaise and mustard, stirring well. Spread 1 tablespoon mayonnaise mixture over bottom of hollowed out portion of each roll; top evenly with beef. Spoon onion mixture over beef; cover with tops of rolls. Serve immediately.
Yield: 4 servings.

Per Serving: Calories 330 (22% from fat)   Fat 7.9g (Sat 2.3g)   Protein 19.7g Carbohydrate 46.2g   Fiber 5.5g   Cholesterol 48mg   Sodium 858mg

Stromboli

Prep: 15 minutes   Cook: 12 minutes

Vegetable cooking spray
½ cup chopped onion
1 (10-ounce) can refrigerated pizza crust dough
2 tablespoons coarse-grained mustard
1 cup (4 ounces) shredded part-skim mozzarella cheese
6 ounces thinly sliced reduced-fat, low-salt ham
1 teaspoon dried Italian seasoning

1 Coat a small nonstick skillet with cooking spray; place over medium-high heat until hot. Add onion, and sauté 4 minutes or until onion is tender; set aside.

2 Unroll dough on a baking sheet coated with cooking spray; press into a 12- x 8-inch rectangle. Spread mustard over dough to within ½ inch of edges. Arrange cheese, onion, and ham lengthwise down center of dough, leaving a ½-inch border at both ends. Sprinkle seasoning over ham.

3 At 1-inch intervals on long sides of rectangle, cut slits from edge of ham to edge of dough. Alternating sides, fold strips at an angle across filling. Coat top of dough with cooking spray. Bake at 425° for 12 to 14 minutes or until browned.
Yield: 5 servings.

Per Serving: Calories 258 (28% from fat)   Fat 8.1g (Sat 3.2g)   Protein 17.0g
Carbohydrate 29.3g   Fiber 1.2g   Cholesterol 30mg   Sodium 763mg

Sandwich Savvy

Impress your family by giving this stromboli sandwich a lattice look. (If you're in a hurry, omit this step and fold the sides over the filling without making the strips.)

Layer the cheese, onion, and ham on the dough rectangle.

Cut 12 strips on both long sides of the rectangle starting at the ham and going to the edge of the dough.

Fold the dough strips at an angle across the filling, alternating strips from each side of the rectangle.

■ Just three high-flavor ingredients—Madeira wine, mango chutney, and lime juice—make a delicious sauce that perfectly complements the flavors of the pork and onion.

Chutney-Pork Sandwiches

Prep: 10 minutes   Cook: 16 minutes

Vegetable cooking spray
1 (¾-pound) pork tenderloin, cut into ¼-inch-thick slices
1 large purple onion, cut in half and sliced
⅓ cup mango chutney
¼ cup Madeira wine
1 tablespoon lime juice
4 (2-ounce) onion rolls, warmed

1 Coat a large nonstick skillet with cooking spray. Place over medium heat until hot. Add pork and onion; cook 10 minutes or until pork is browned and onion is crisp-tender, stirring often. Add chutney, wine, and lime juice. Cook over medium heat 6 minutes or until pork is tender. Spoon over bottom halves of rolls. Top with remaining roll halves. Serve warm.
Yield: 4 servings.

Per Serving: Calories 352 (13% from fat)   Fat 5.2g (Sat 2.2g)   Protein 23.6g   Carbohydrate 50.7g   Fiber 2.1g   Cholesterol 55mg   Sodium 540mg

■ This sandwich is like a French bread pizza. It can also be an appetizer if you cut each sandwich into thin slices.

Ham and Mushroom Melt

Prep: 20 minutes   Cook: 2 minutes

1 (8-ounce) loaf French bread
1 large clove garlic, split
½ teaspoon freshly ground pepper
Olive oil-flavored vegetable cooking spray
2 teaspoons reduced-calorie margarine
2 (8-ounce) packages sliced fresh mushrooms
4 ounces thinly sliced reduced-fat, low-salt ham, cut into thin strips
½ teaspoon chopped fresh thyme
3 ounces provolone cheese, thinly sliced

1 Cut bread in half horizontally. Rub garlic over cut sides of bread; sprinkle with pepper. Place on a baking sheet, cut sides up. Broil 5½ inches from heat (with electric oven door partially opened) 3 minutes.

2 Coat a nonstick skillet with cooking spray; add margarine. Place over medium-high heat until margarine melts. Add mushrooms; sauté 8 minutes. Arrange mushrooms over bread; top with ham. Sprinkle with thyme; top with cheese. Broil 5½ inches from heat 2 minutes or until cheese melts. Cut each bread half into 2 pieces.
Yield: 4 servings.

Per Serving: Calories 313 (28% from fat)   Fat 9.9g (Sat 4.7g)   Protein 18.1g   Carbohydrate 37.9g   Fiber 2.9g   Cholesterol 30mg   Sodium 757mg

Skillet Chicken Pitas

Prep: 5 minutes   Cook: 16 minutes

⅓ cup nonfat mayonnaise
¼ teaspoon garlic powder
2 (8-inch) pita bread rounds
6 ounces cooked chicken breast, cut into strips (skinned before
      cooking and cooked without salt or fat)
1 cup shredded iceberg lettuce
¾ cup chopped tomato
⅓ cup peeled, coarsely chopped cucumber
Vegetable cooking spray
¼ cup water, divided

1 Combine mayonnaise and garlic powder. Separate each pita round into 2 rounds. Spread mayonnaise mixture evenly on inside of split rounds. Arrange chicken strips evenly down centers of pita rounds; top evenly with lettuce, tomato, and cucumber. Fold over left and right sides of pita rounds to partially enclose filling. Fold short sides over to form rectangles.

2 Coat a nonstick skillet with cooking spray. Place over medium-high heat until hot. Sprinkle 1 tablespoon water in skillet. Place 2 sandwiches, seam sides down, in skillet; press firmly. Cook 2 to 3 minutes or until lightly browned. Turn sandwiches; press firmly, and cook 2 additional minutes or until lightly browned. Wrap in wax paper, and keep warm. Repeat procedure.
Yield: 4 servings.

Per Serving: Calories 191 (9% from fat)   Fat 1.9g (Sat 0.5g)   Protein 13.2g   Carbohydrate 27.7g   Fiber 4.5g   Cholesterol 29mg   Sodium 600mg

■ One large chicken breast half or two small ones will give you about 6 ounces of cooked chicken. (Or you can use roasted chicken from the grocery store deli.)

Pita Prep

Fold left and right sides of pita over the chicken and vegetables to partially enclose the mixture.

Fold the short sides in to form a rectangular package.

Place the sandwiches in the skillet, seam sides down, and cook until lightly browned.

For crisp turkey bacon, cook it in the microwave at HIGH for 1 minute per slice.

Club Sandwiches

Prep: 15 minutes

¼ cup fat-free Thousand Island dressing
8 (1-ounce) slices whole wheat bread, toasted
4 green leaf lettuce leaves
8 slices tomato
4 ounces thinly sliced cooked turkey breast
4 (¾-ounce) slices fat-free sharp Cheddar cheese
4 slices turkey bacon, cooked and cut in half

1 Spread 1 tablespoon dressing over one side of each of 4 bread slices. Arrange lettuce and remaining 4 ingredients evenly over dressing on slices; top with remaining bread slices. Cut each sandwich into 4 triangles. Secure sandwiches with wooden picks.
Yield: 4 servings. *(Recipe pictured on page 188.)*

Per Serving: Calories 282 (15% from fat) Fat 4.8g (Sat 1.1g) Protein 21.9g Carbohydrate 38.2g Fiber 3.3g Cholesterol 34mg Sodium 982mg

Red, yellow, and orange peppers make nice color and flavor variations, but they're usually more expensive than the green ones.

Sausage-Pepper Buns

Prep: 15 minutes   Cook: 10 minutes

Vegetable cooking spray
1 (14-ounce) package fat-free smoked turkey sausage, sliced
1 teaspoon reduced-calorie margarine
2 medium-size green peppers, seeded and sliced
1 large onion, sliced
1 teaspoon salt-free Greek seasoning
6 whole wheat hot dog buns

1 Coat a large nonstick skillet with cooking spray; place over medium-high heat until hot. Add sausage, and cook 5 minutes or until browned, stirring often. Remove from skillet, and set aside. Wipe skillet dry with a paper towel.

2 Coat skillet with cooking spray; add margarine. Place over medium-high heat until margarine melts. Add green pepper and onion; sauté 8 minutes or until vegetables are tender. Return sausage to skillet; sprinkle Greek seasoning over sausage. Cook 1 minute or until thoroughly heated, stirring occasionally. Spoon sausage mixture evenly into buns. Serve warm.
Yield: 6 servings.

Per Serving: Calories 249 (16% from fat) Fat 4.5g (Sat 0.7g) Protein 14.8g Carbohydrate 37.0g Fiber 1.8g Cholesterol 44mg Sodium 931mg

Italian-Seasoned Snack Mix

Prep: 10 minutes   Cook: 25 minutes

4 cups crispy corn-and-rice cereal (such as Crispix)
2 cups oyster crackers
2 cups small fat-free pretzels
¼ cup reduced-calorie margarine, melted
2 egg whites, lightly beaten
¼ cup grated Parmesan cheese
1 tablespoon dried Italian seasoning
Vegetable cooking spray

1 Combine first 3 ingredients in a large bowl. Combine margarine and egg whites in a small bowl, stirring well with a wire whisk. Pour margarine mixture over cereal mixture; toss lightly to coat. Sprinkle with cheese and Italian seasoning; toss lightly.

2 Spread mixture in 2 (15- x 10- x 1-inch) jellyroll pans coated with cooking spray. Bake at 300° for 25 minutes or until crisp, stirring occasionally. Cool completely. Store in an airtight container.
Yield: 24 (¼-cup) servings.

Per Serving: Calories 62 (29% from fat)   Fat 2.0g (Sat 0.3g)   Protein 1.6g
Carbohydrate 9.9g   Fiber 0.5g   Cholesterol 1mg   Sodium 188mg

■ The egg white helps moisten the cereal mixture and creates a crispy coating on the mixture as it cooks.

Spicy Pepper Pita Chips

Prep: 10 minutes   Cook: 15 minutes

3 (7-inch) pita bread rounds
Olive oil-flavored vegetable cooking spray
1½ tablespoons salt-free spicy pepper seasoning
¼ teaspoon salt

1 Cut each pita round into 12 wedges. Coat both sides of wedges with cooking spray.

2 Combine seasoning and salt in a large heavy-duty, zip-top plastic bag; shake well. Add 6 pita wedges to bag; secure bag, and shake to coat wedges. Remove wedges from bag. Repeat procedure five times with remaining wedges and seasoning mixture. Place wedges on a baking sheet coated with cooking spray. Bake at 300° for 15 to 20 minutes or until lightly browned and crisp.
Yield: 36 chips.

Per Chip: Calories 18 (15% from fat)   Fat 0.3g (Sat 0.1g)   Protein 0.4g
Carbohydrate 3.2g   Fiber 0.5g   Cholesterol 0mg   Sodium 31mg

■ For thinner, crispier chips, split each pita round in half horizontally. Cut each round into 12 wedges for a total of 72 chips. Double the pepper seasoning and salt to sprinkle over the chips.

Caramel-Apple Crisp

Caramel-Apple Crisps

Prep: 9 minutes

6 (4-inch) fat-free caramel-flavored popcorn cakes
1 Golden or Red Delicious apple, thinly sliced
1½ tablespoons fat-free caramel-flavored syrup
1 tablespoon brown sugar
½ teaspoon ground cinnamon

1 Place popcorn cakes on a baking sheet. Top evenly with sliced apple; drizzle caramel syrup evenly over apple. Combine brown sugar and cinnamon. Sprinkle over each serving. Broil 5½ inches from heat (with electric oven door partially opened) 3 minutes. Serve immediately.
Yield: 6 servings.

Per Serving: Calories 84 (1% from fat) Fat 0.1g (Sat 0.0g) Protein 1.1g Carbohydrate 20.6g Fiber 0.8g Cholesterol 0mg Sodium 40mg

■ For variety, use whatever fruit suits your taste. Banana slices and pear slices are delicious with the caramel syrup.

Tropical S'mores

Prep: 15 minutes

¼ cup drained canned crushed pineapple in juice
¼ cup peeled, seeded, and chopped papaya
1 teaspoon fresh lime juice
4 (4¾- x 2½-inch) low-fat graham crackers
½ cup miniature marshmallows
2 teaspoons flaked coconut

1 Combine first 3 ingredients in a small bowl.

2 Place graham crackers on a baking sheet; top evenly with marshmallows, pineapple mixture, and coconut. Broil 3 inches from heat (with electric oven door partially opened) 40 seconds or until topping is lightly browned. Serve immediately.
Yield: 4 servings.

Per Serving: Calories 116 (7% from fat) Fat 0.9g (Sat 0.5g) Protein 1.3g Carbohydrate 26.2g Fiber 0.9g Cholesterol 0mg Sodium 105mg

■ Maybe you remember making s'mores as a kid— crispy graham crackers, toasted marshmallows, and melted chocolate bars. Here's a tropical (and slightly healthier) version.

■ Use nonfat cream cheese from a tub because it's a little softer and easier to spread than the nonfat cream cheese in a block.

Mini Garlic Pizzas

Prep: 15 minutes

½ cup nonfat cream cheese, softened
2 teaspoons minced fresh basil
1 teaspoon commercial roasted minced garlic
¼ cup grated Parmesan cheese, divided
5 miniature bagels, split and toasted
1 large plum tomato, cut into 10 slices

1 Combine first 3 ingredients in a small bowl. Add 3 tablespoons Parmesan cheese, and stir well. Spread 1 tablespoon cheese mixture over cut side of each bagel half; top each with a tomato slice. Sprinkle evenly with remaining 1 tablespoon Parmesan cheese.
Yield: 10 servings.

Per Serving: Calories 48 (17% from fat)   Fat 0.9g (Sat 0.4g)   Protein 2.5g   Carbohydrate 7.6g   Fiber 0.4g   Cholesterol 2mg   Sodium 115mg

■ Serve these two-cheese pizza crust sticks (with or without the sauce) with soups and salads.

Pepper-Cheese Pizza Sticks

Prep: 15 minutes   Cook: 8 minutes

1 (10-ounce) can refrigerated pizza crust dough
Vegetable cooking spray
1 tablespoon margarine, melted
½ cup (2 ounces) shredded reduced-fat sharp Cheddar cheese
1 tablespoon grated Parmesan cheese
1 teaspoon cracked black pepper
¼ teaspoon ground red pepper
1 cup low-fat spaghetti sauce with garlic and herbs

1 Unroll dough on a large baking sheet coated with cooking spray. Press dough into a 12- x 9-inch rectangle. Brush melted margarine over dough. Sprinkle with Cheddar cheese and next 3 ingredients. Cut dough crosswise into 12 (1-inch-wide) strips, using a sharp knife or a pizza cutter. Cut dough in half lengthwise, forming 24 strips. (Do not separate strips.) Bake at 425° for 8 to 10 minutes or until golden. To separate sticks, cut along perforations.

2 Place spaghetti sauce in a small saucepan. Cook over medium heat until thoroughly heated. Serve with pizza sticks.
Yield: 8 servings (serving size: 3 sticks plus 1 tablespoon sauce).

Per Serving: Calories 141 (28% from fat)   Fat 4.4g (Sat 1.4g)   Protein 5.9g   Carbohydrate 19.5g   Fiber 1.1g   Cholesterol 5mg   Sodium 372mg

Creamy Pineapple Pops

Prep: 10 minutes   Freeze: 2 hours

1 (15¼-ounce) can crushed pineapple, undrained
1 (8-ounce) carton low-fat pineapple yogurt
3 tablespoons honey
1 tablespoon chopped fresh mint (optional)
6 (6-ounce) paper cups
6 wooden sticks

1 Combine first 3 ingredients in a small bowl. Stir in mint, if desired.

2 Spoon pineapple mixture evenly into paper cups. Cover tops of cups with aluminum foil, and insert a wooden stick through foil into center of each cup. Freeze until firm. To serve, remove aluminum foil; peel cup from pop.
Yield: 6 servings.

Per Serving: Calories 113 (4% from fat)   Fat 0.5g (Sat 0.3g)   Protein 1.8g Carbohydrate 27.1g   Fiber 0.6g   Cholesterol 2mg   Sodium 21mg

■ For kid appeal, use fun-shaped popsicle molds instead of paper cups and wooden sticks.

Strawberries 'n' Cream Pops

Prep: 10 minutes   Freeze: 2 hours

1 (8-ounce) carton plain nonfat yogurt
1 (8-ounce) package nonfat cream cheese
2 (10-ounce) packages frozen sweetened strawberries, thawed
8 (6-ounce) paper cups
8 wooden sticks

1 Place yogurt and cream cheese in container of an electric blender. Cover and process until smooth, stopping once to scrape down sides. Add strawberries, and process until smooth.

2 Spoon strawberry mixture evenly into paper cups. Cover tops of cups with aluminum foil, and insert a wooden stick through foil into center of each cup. Freeze until firm. To serve, remove aluminum foil; peel cup from pop.
Yield: 8 servings.

Per Serving: Calories 68 (1% from fat)   Fat 0.1g (Sat 0.0g)   Protein 5.8g Carbohydrate 10.6g   Fiber 0.2g   Cholesterol 6mg   Sodium 192mg

■ Need rescuing on a rainy day? Let the kids decorate the wooden sticks and insert them into the cups.

Side Dishes

A side dish is supposed to be a simple addition to the main portion of the meal. The key word is simple. If I'm making a quick and easy entrée, why should I fret over what to serve on the side?

Fruits and vegetables make great side dishes because they require so little prep time. And you don't have to do much to fresh produce to make it taste good. When you use my suggestions for steaming, sautéing, and stewing fresh fruits and vegetables, your side dishes might become the feature attractions.

Nutty Asparagus (page 210)

You can substitute fresh apples for the canned ones. Use 6 cups peeled, sliced apple plus 1 cup unsweetened apple juice.

Tart Spiced Apples

Prep: 5 minutes   Cook: 20 minutes

2 (20-ounce) cans sliced apples
1½ tablespoons lemon juice
¼ cup firmly packed brown sugar
2 tablespoons reduced-calorie margarine
1 teaspoon apple pie spice

1 Drain apple slices, reserving juice. Add water to juice to equal 1 cup; set aside. Combine apple slices and lemon juice; toss lightly.

2 Combine apple slices, apple juice mixture, brown sugar, margarine, and apple pie spice in a large saucepan. Bring to a boil. Reduce heat, and simmer, uncovered, 20 to 25 minutes or until apple is tender, stirring occasionally. Serve warm.
Yield: 4 (1-cup) servings.

Per Serving: Calories 135 (25% from fat)   Fat 3.7g (Sat 0.5g)   Protein 0.1g   Carbohydrate 26.3g   Fiber 2.1g   Cholesterol 0mg   Sodium 81mg

Serve this sweet side dish with pork or chicken. Or turn it into a dessert by topping it with a scoop of low-fat vanilla ice cream.

Honeyed Bananas

Prep: 6 minutes   Cook: 3 minutes

6 medium bananas
2 tablespoons lemon juice
½ teaspoon ground cinnamon
2 tablespoons reduced-calorie margarine
3 tablespoons honey

1 Peel bananas, and brush with lemon juice. Sprinkle bananas with cinnamon.

2 Melt margarine in a large nonstick skillet over medium heat; stir in honey. Add bananas, and cook 3 to 4 minutes or until bananas are thoroughly heated, turning once. Serve immediately.
Yield: 6 servings.

Per Serving: Calories 152 (17% from fat)   Fat 2.9g (Sat 0.5g)   Protein 1.1g   Carbohydrate 34.2g   Fiber 3.2g   Cholesterol 0mg   Sodium 38mg

Grilled Pineapple

Prep: 15 minutes   Stand: 45 minutes   Cook: 4 minutes

1 medium-size fresh pineapple, peeled and cored
¼ cup reduced-sodium teriyaki sauce
2 tablespoons brown sugar
2 teaspoons vegetable oil
Vegetable cooking spray

1 Cut pineapple crosswise into 8 slices; place in a 13- x 9- x 2-inch baking dish. Combine teriyaki sauce, sugar, and oil, stirring well. Pour teriyaki mixture over pineapple, turning pineapple to coat. Let stand at room temperature 45 minutes, turning pineapple once. Remove pineapple from marinade; discard marinade.

2 Coat grill rack with cooking spray; place on grill over medium-hot coals (350° to 400°). Place pineapple on rack; grill, covered, 2 minutes on each side or until pineapple is tender.
Yield: 8 servings.

Per Serving: Calories 56 (16% from fat)   Fat 1.0g (Sat 0.1g)   Protein 0.4g
Carbohydrate 12.0g   Fiber 1.3g   Cholesterol 0mg   Sodium 81mg

■ To make prep time even quicker, buy a peeled, cored fresh pineapple.

Grilled Pineapple

If you don't have walnuts on hand, use cashews or pecans.

Nutty Asparagus
Prep: 6 minutes   Cook: 20 minutes

1 pound fresh asparagus spears
Vegetable cooking spray
1 tablespoon lemon juice
2 teaspoons reduced-calorie margarine, melted
1½ tablespoons coarsely chopped walnuts
¼ teaspoon salt
⅛ teaspoon freshly ground pepper

1 Snap off tough ends of asparagus. Remove scales from stalks with a knife or vegetable peeler, if desired. Place asparagus in an 8-inch square baking dish coated with cooking spray.

2 Combine lemon juice and margarine; brush over asparagus. Sprinkle nuts, salt, and pepper over asparagus. Bake, uncovered, at 350° for 20 minutes or until asparagus is tender.
Yield: 4 servings.   *(Recipe pictured on page 206.)*

Per Serving: Calories 48 (56% from fat)   Fat 3.0g (Sat 0.3g)   Protein 2.6g Carbohydrate 4.5g   Fiber 2.0g   Cholesterol 0mg   Sodium 167mg

It takes about 2 slices of whole wheat bread to make 1 cup of soft breadcrumbs.

Broccoli Casserole
Prep: 10 minutes   Cook: 30 minutes

2 (10-ounce) packages frozen chopped broccoli
1 (10¾-ounce) can reduced-fat, reduced-sodium cream of celery
       (or mushroom) soup
1 (8-ounce) can sliced water chestnuts, drained
1 (4-ounce) can sliced mushrooms, drained
¼ teaspoon salt
⅛ teaspoon pepper
Vegetable cooking spray
1 cup soft whole wheat breadcrumbs
⅔ cup (2.6 ounces) shredded reduced-fat sharp Cheddar cheese
1 tablespoon reduced-calorie margarine, melted

1 Cook broccoli according to package directions; drain.

2 Combine broccoli, soup, and next 4 ingredients. Spoon into a 1½-quart baking dish coated with cooking spray. Combine bread-crumbs, cheese, and margarine. Sprinkle crumb mixture over broccoli mixture. Bake at 350° for 30 minutes.
Yield: 8 servings.

Per Serving: Calories 112 (31% from fat)   Fat 3.8g (Sat 1.4g)   Protein 6.3g Carbohydrate 14.8g   Fiber 2.5g   Cholesterol 7mg   Sodium 378mg

Citrus Cabbage Grill

Prep: 10 minutes   Cook: 35 minutes

¼ cup plus 2 tablespoons frozen citrus beverage concentrate
    (such as Five-Alive), thawed and undiluted
¼ cup water
1 tablespoon olive oil
1 teaspoon salt
½ teaspoon celery seeds
½ teaspoon mustard seeds
½ teaspoon pepper
1 large cabbage, cut into 8 wedges

1 Combine first 7 ingredients, stirring well.

2 Cut 8 (12-inch) squares of heavy-duty aluminum foil. Place a cabbage wedge on each square of foil. Bring edges of foil up, but do not seal. Pour juice mixture evenly over cabbage, and seal packets.

3 Place grill rack on grill over medium-hot coals (350° to 400°). Place foil packets on rack; grill, covered, 35 minutes or until cabbage is tender.
Yield: 8 servings.

Note: To bake cabbage, place wedges in a 13- x 9- x 2-inch baking dish. Pour juice mixture over cabbage. Cover and bake at 375° for 1 hour and 10 minutes or until cabbage is tender.

Per Serving: Calories 73 (27% from fat)   Fat 2.2g (Sat 0.3g)   Protein 2.7g
Carbohydrate 12.7g   Fiber 5.1g   Cholesterol 0mg   Sodium 331mg

It's a Wrap

Place a cabbage wedge in the center of the foil square.

Make a bowl around the cabbage with the foil, and add the liquid mixture.

Seal the packet tightly around the cabbage.

Crystallized ginger is fresh ginger that has been cooked in a sugar syrup and coated with coarse sugar. It adds a sweeter ginger flavor than fresh gingerroot and can be used in savory dishes as well as in desserts.

Apricot-Ginger Carrots

Prep: 2 minutes   Cook: 20 minutes

1 (2-pound) package fresh baby carrots
1 cup water
1 (10-ounce) jar low-sugar apricot preserves
2 tablespoons margarine
2 teaspoons minced crystallized ginger

1 Combine carrots and water in a medium saucepan; bring to a boil. Cover, reduce heat, and simmer 12 minutes or until carrots are tender. Drain and transfer carrots to a bowl.

2 Combine preserves, margarine, and ginger in saucepan. Cook over low heat, stirring constantly, 2 minutes or until preserves melt. Return carrots to saucepan; toss lightly. Cook until thoroughly heated. Serve with a slotted spoon.
Yield: 10 (½-cup) servings.

Per Serving: Calories 126 (17% from fat)   Fat 2.4g (Sat 0.5g)   Protein 0.9g
Carbohydrate 25.8g   Fiber 2.9g   Cholesterol 0mg   Sodium 59mg

When fresh green beans are in season, trim 1 pound of beans, and cut into 1-inch pieces. Steam them for 6 minutes or until they're done.

Italian Green Beans

Prep: 15 minutes   Cook: 10 minutes

1 (16-ounce) package frozen Italian-cut green beans
Vegetable cooking spray
1 teaspoon olive oil
¼ cup chopped onion
¼ cup chopped green pepper
1 clove garlic, minced
1 (14½-ounce) can no-salt-added diced tomatoes, undrained
¼ teaspoon dried Italian seasoning
¼ teaspoon salt
2 tablespoons freshly grated Parmesan cheese

1 Cook green beans according to package directions, omitting salt and fat. Set aside, and keep warm.

2 Coat a nonstick skillet with cooking spray; add oil. Place over medium-high heat until hot. Add onion, green pepper, and garlic; sauté 4 minutes. Stir in tomato, Italian seasoning, and salt. Cook until thoroughly heated, stirring often. Combine green beans and tomato mixture; toss lightly. Sprinkle with Parmesan cheese.
Yield: 4 (1-cup) servings.

Per Serving: Calories 100 (22% from fat)   Fat 2.4g (Sat 0.8g)   Protein 5.1g
Carbohydrate 17.7g   Fiber 4.6g   Cholesterol 2mg   Sodium 226mg

Stewed Okra, Corn, and Tomatoes

Prep: 5 minutes   Cook: 20 minutes

1½ cups frozen sliced okra
1 cup frozen whole-kernel corn
¼ cup chopped reduced-fat, low-salt ham
1 (14½-ounce) can no-salt-added stewed tomatoes, undrained
1 teaspoon dried basil
¼ teaspoon salt
¼ teaspoon pepper
Vegetable cooking spray

1 Combine first 7 ingredients in a large saucepan coated with cooking spray. Bring to a boil; cover, reduce heat, and simmer 15 minutes, stirring occasionally.
Yield: 4 (¾-cup) servings.

Per Serving: Calories 88 (8% from fat)   Fat 0.8g (Sat 0.2g)   Protein 4.7g
Carbohydrate 17.7g   Fiber 2.1g   Cholesterol 4mg   Sodium 238mg

■ This is basically a dump and cook recipe. There's no need to thaw the okra or corn before combining all the ingredients. They'll thaw as the mixture cooks.

Stewed Okra, Corn, and Tomatoes

■ Vary the flavor slightly by using another flavored vegetable oil like chile or herb. The flavored oils are on the grocery shelf next to the plain vegetable oils. Or use olive oil or regular vegetable oil.

Pepper Sauté

Prep: 7 minutes   Cook: 5 minutes

2 teaspoons roasted garlic-flavored vegetable oil
1 medium-size green pepper, cut into strips
1 medium-size sweet red pepper, cut into strips
1 medium-size sweet yellow pepper, cut into strips
1 medium onion, cut into eighths
1 (8-ounce) package sliced fresh mushrooms
1 teaspoon dried Italian seasoning
¼ teaspoon salt
¼ teaspoon freshly ground pepper

1 Heat oil in a large nonstick skillet over medium-high heat until hot. Add pepper strips and remaining ingredients; sauté 5 to 7 minutes or until crisp-tender.
Yield: 6 (1-cup) servings.

Per Serving: Calories 56 (34% from fat)   Fat 2.1g (Sat 0.4g)   Protein 1.8g   Carbohydrate 8.9g   Fiber 2.4g   Cholesterol 0mg   Sodium 103mg

■ If you have some fresh gingerroot left over, wrap it tightly in heavy-duty plastic wrap, and store it in the refrigerator for a week or in the freezer for up to two months.

Sesame Sugar Snap Peas

Prep: 15 minutes

Vegetable cooking spray
1 teaspoon dark sesame oil
2 (8-ounce) packages frozen Sugar Snap peas
1 (8-ounce) can sliced water chestnuts, drained
¼ cup low-sodium soy sauce
3 tablespoons brown sugar
1 tablespoon peeled, chopped gingerroot
2 teaspoons cornstarch

1 Coat a large nonstick skillet with cooking spray; add oil. Place over medium-high heat until hot. Add peas and water chestnuts; sauté 4 to 5 minutes or until peas are crisp-tender.

2 Combine soy sauce and remaining 3 ingredients, stirring until smooth. Add to vegetable mixture. Bring to a boil, and cook, stirring constantly, 2 minutes or until thickened and bubbly.
Yield: 6 (¾-cup) servings.

Per Serving: Calories 90 (11% from fat)   Fat 1.1g (Sat 0.1g)   Protein 2.4g   Carbohydrate 16.7g   Fiber 2.2g   Cholesterol 0mg   Sodium 268mg

Cheddar Scalloped Potatoes

Prep: 10 minutes   Cook: 15 minutes

1 pound baking potatoes, cut into ¼-inch-thick slices
4 green onions, thinly sliced
Vegetable cooking spray
1½ teaspoons reduced-calorie margarine
1 tablespoon all-purpose flour
⅛ teaspoon salt
⅛ teaspoon ground red pepper
1 cup skim milk
⅓ cup (1.3 ounces) shredded reduced-fat sharp Cheddar cheese

1 Arrange potato and onions in an 8-inch square baking dish. Cover with heavy-duty plastic wrap, and vent. Microwave at HIGH 10 minutes or until potato is tender, stirring every 4 minutes. Set aside.

2 Coat a 2-cup glass measure with cooking spray; add margarine. Microwave at HIGH 30 seconds or until margarine melts. Add flour, salt, and pepper; stir well. Add milk, stirring until smooth. Microwave at HIGH 3 minutes or until thickened, stirring with a wire whisk every 1½ minutes. Add cheese; microwave at HIGH 30 seconds or until cheese melts. Pour cheese mixture over potato and onions; stir. Microwave at HIGH 1 minute or until thoroughly heated.
Yield: 4 servings. *(Potatoes pictured on page 16.)*

Per Serving: Calories 192 (15% from fat) Fat 3.1g (Sat 1.3g) Protein 7.6g
Carbohydrate 34.0g Fiber 2.3g Cholesterol 7mg Sodium 193mg

■ Cheddar cheese adds the sharpest flavor to these creamy potatoes, but they're also good with reduced-fat Swiss or Monterey Jack.

Sweet Potatoes in Orange Syrup

Prep: 15 minutes   Cook: 35 minutes

2¼ pounds sweet potatoes, peeled and cut into ¼-inch-thick slices
Butter-flavored vegetable cooking spray
¼ cup reduced-calorie maple syrup
1 tablespoon frozen orange juice concentrate, undiluted
2 tablespoons coarsely chopped pecans, toasted

1 Place potato, overlapping slightly, on a jellyroll pan coated with cooking spray. Coat potato with cooking spray. Bake, uncovered, at 375° for 30 minutes or until tender, turning once. Transfer to a bowl.

2 Combine syrup, juice concentrate, and pecans in a glass measure. Microwave at HIGH 30 seconds; drizzle over potato slices.
Yield: 6 (⅔-cup) servings.

Per Serving: Calories 188 (12% from fat) Fat 2.6g (Sat 0.2g) Protein 2.7g
Carbohydrate 39.7g Fiber 4.7g Cholesterol 0mg Sodium 22mg

■ These glazed sweet potatoes will fit right into a holiday turkey-and-dressing meal or a roasted pork or baked chicken dinner.

Stuffing a Squash

Scoop out the pulp from the cooked squash using a melon baller or a small spoon.

Invert the squash shells onto paper towels to drain excess moisture.

Stuffed Yellow Squash

Prep: 20 minutes   Cook: 4 minutes

4 medium-size yellow squash
Olive oil-flavored vegetable cooking spray
¼ cup minced green onions
2 tablespoons finely chopped sweet red pepper
2 tablespoons finely chopped green pepper
¾ cup frozen whole-kernel corn, thawed
⅓ cup crumbled feta cheese
¼ teaspoon salt
¼ teaspoon freshly ground pepper
Green onion curl (optional)

1 Pierce squash several times with a fork. Place squash in microwave oven on paper towels. Microwave, uncovered, at HIGH 4 minutes, rearranging squash after 2 minutes. Let stand 5 minutes.

2 Cut each squash in half lengthwise; scoop out and discard pulp, leaving ¼-inch-thick shells. Invert squash shells onto paper towels, and set aside.

3 Coat a small nonstick skillet with cooking spray; place over medium-high heat until hot. Add minced green onions and chopped pepper; sauté until tender. Remove from heat; add corn and next 3 ingredients.

4 Spoon vegetable mixture evenly into squash shells. Place stuffed shells in a 13- x 9- x 2-inch baking dish coated with cooking spray. Cover with heavy-duty plastic wrap and vent. Microwave at HIGH 4 to 6 minutes or until thoroughly heated. Place squash on a serving platter. Garnish with a green onion curl, if desired.
Yield: 4 servings.

Note: If a 13- x 9- x 2-inch baking dish will not fit in your microwave oven, bake in a conventional oven at 350° for 15 to 20 minutes or until thoroughly heated.

Per Serving: Calories 88 (31% from fat)   Fat 3.0g (Sat 1.7g)   Protein 4.2g   Carbohydrate 13.7g   Fiber 3.5g   Cholesterol 9mg   Sodium 270mg

Stuffed Yellow Squash

Acorn squash is a winter squash with dark green ribbed skin and orange flesh. It's available year-round, but is best from early fall through winter. Other varieties of winter squash include butternut, spaghetti squash, and pumpkin.

Orange-Streusel Acorn Squash

Prep: 40 minutes   Cook: 15 minutes

2 small acorn squash (about ¾ pound each)
¼ cup frozen orange juice concentrate, thawed and undiluted
2 tablespoons brown sugar
¼ teaspoon ground allspice
Vegetable cooking spray
⅓ cup corn flake crumbs
1½ tablespoons coarsely chopped pecans
2 teaspoons reduced-calorie margarine, melted

1 Wash squash; cut in half crosswise. Remove and discard seeds. Place squash, cut sides down, in a 13- x 9- x 2-inch baking dish. Add hot water to dish to depth of ½ inch. Bake, uncovered, at 400° for 30 to 40 minutes or until tender. Drain and let cool slightly.

2 Scoop out pulp into a bowl, leaving ¼-inch-thick shells. Mash pulp. Add orange juice concentrate, brown sugar, and allspice; stir well. Cut a thin slice off bottom of each squash shell so it will sit flat. Coat baking dish with cooking spray; return squash shells to baking dish. Spoon squash mixture evenly into shells.

3 Combine corn flake crumbs, pecans, and margarine. Sprinkle crumb mixture evenly over squash. Bake, uncovered, at 400° for 15 to 20 minutes or until thoroughly heated.
Yield: 4 servings.

Per Serving: Calories 155 (19% from fat)   Fat 3.3g (Sat 0.4g)   Protein 2.3g Carbohydrate 31.7g   Fiber 2.0g   Cholesterol 0mg   Sodium 113mg

Baked Butternut Squash

Prep: 5 minutes   Bake: 1 hour and 5 minutes

1 medium butternut squash (about 2 pounds)
⅓ cup mango chutney
1 teaspoon peeled, grated gingerroot
¼ teaspoon freshly grated nutmeg (or ground nutmeg)

1 Wash squash; cut in half lengthwise. Remove and discard seeds.
Place squash, cut sides up, in an 11- x 7- x 1½-inch baking dish.
Combine chutney, gingerroot, and nutmeg. Brush some of the chut-
ney mixture over cut sides of squash; spoon remaining mixture into
cavities of squash. Cover and bake at 400° for 1 hour or until tender.
Remove from oven; brush with chutney mixture remaining in dish.
Broil 5½ inches from heat (with electric oven door partially opened)
5 minutes or until browned.
Yield: 4 servings (serving size: ½ squash half).

Per Serving: Calories 154 (2% from fat)   Fat 0.3g (Sat 0.1g)   Protein 2.5g
Carbohydrate 39.6g   Fiber 2.8g   Cholesterol 0mg   Sodium 54mg

■ The freshly grated nutmeg
adds a warm, spicy, and sweet
flavor to the squash. Grate
nutmeg with a nutmeg grater
or grinder (found in specialty
kitchenware shops). For a
coarser grind, use a hand-held
cheese grater. Look for fresh
nutmeg in the spice section
of the grocery store.

Pan-Fried Dill Tomatoes

Prep: 20 minutes

1 cup peeled, diced cucumber (about 1 medium)
1 tablespoon cider vinegar
¾ cup fine, dry breadcrumbs
3 tablespoons grated Parmesan cheese
2 tablespoons chopped fresh dillweed
¼ teaspoon freshly ground pepper
⅛ teaspoon salt
2 tablespoons water
2 egg whites, lightly beaten
10 (½-inch-thick) slices tomato (about 3 medium tomatoes)
Olive oil-flavored vegetable cooking spray

1 Combine cucumber and vinegar; set aside. Combine breadcrumbs
and next 4 ingredients. Combine water and egg whites, stirring well
with a wire whisk. Dredge tomato slices in breadcrumb mixture, and
dip in egg white mixture. Dredge in breadcrumb mixture again.

2 Heavily coat a large nonstick skillet with cooking spray. Place over
medium-high heat until hot. Add tomato; cook 1 minute on each
side or until golden. Serve warm with cucumber mixture.
Yield: 5 servings.

Per Serving: Calories 115 (20% from fat)   Fat 2.5g (Sat 0.8g)   Protein 5.9g
Carbohydrate 18.6g   Fiber 2.5g   Cholesterol 2mg   Sodium 282mg

■ The substitution for 2
tablespoons fresh dillweed is
2 teaspoons dried dillweed.

Soups

A bowl of soup. The very words soothe and comfort me. But that's not all; they relax me, too. What could be easier than blending a mixture of fruit or vegetables to a creamy consistency, or tossing a few hearty, tasty ingredients into a pot and letting the stove do all the work?

Whether it is chilled or hot, smooth and creamy or full of chunky vegetables, all I have to do is ladle my meal into a bowl and pull out the crackers or a loaf of French bread.

Springtime Strawberry Soup (page 222)

221

Dollop small amounts of yogurt on top of the soup.

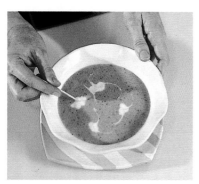

Swirl dollops into designs using a wooden pick.

Springtime Strawberry Soup

Prep: 20 minutes   Chill: 2 hours

5 cups sliced fresh strawberries (2 quarts)
½ cup unsweetened apple juice
2 cups nonfat buttermilk
¼ cup dry red wine
¼ cup sifted powdered sugar
¼ teaspoon ground cinnamon
¼ cup plus 2 tablespoons low-fat vanilla yogurt
Strawberry blossoms (optional)

1 Place strawberries and apple juice in container of an electric blender; cover and process until smooth. Transfer to a bowl. Add buttermilk and next 3 ingredients; stir well. Cover and chill at least 2 hours. Ladle into bowls; top each with 1 tablespoon yogurt, swirling if desired. Garnish with strawberry blossoms, if desired. **Yield: 6 (1-cup) servings.**   *(Recipe pictured on page 220.)*

Per Serving: Calories 113 (7% from fat)   Fat 0.9g (Sat 0.4g)   Protein 4.5g   Carbohydrate 21.6g   Fiber 3.0g   Cholesterol 3mg   Sodium 101mg

Cream of Carrot Soup

Prep: 15 minutes   Cool: 10 minutes   Cook: 25 minutes

Vegetable cooking spray
1 tablespoon margarine
½ cup chopped onion
½ cup sliced celery
1 pound carrots, scraped and thinly sliced
2 cups canned no-salt-added chicken broth
½ cup evaporated skimmed milk
1¼ teaspoons chopped fresh dillweed
¼ teaspoon salt
¼ teaspoon pepper

1 Coat a saucepan with cooking spray. Add margarine; place over medium-high heat until margarine melts. Add onion and celery; sauté until tender. Add carrot and broth. Bring to a boil; cover, reduce heat, and simmer 20 minutes. Remove from heat; cool 10 minutes.

2 Transfer mixture to container of an electric blender; cover and process until smooth. Return to saucepan. Add milk; cook 3 minutes or until thoroughly heated. Stir in dillweed, salt, and pepper. **Yield: 4 (1-cup) servings.**

Per Serving: Calories 110 (27% from fat)   Fat 3.3g (Sat 0.6g)   Protein 3.9g   Carbohydrate 15.8g   Fiber 3.4g   Cholesterol 1mg   Sodium 265mg

Gazpacho

Prep: 20 minutes   Chill: 3 hours

2 cups peeled, chopped cucumber (about 2 medium)
1 cup chopped green pepper (about 1 large)
1 cup chopped sweet red pepper (about 1 large)
1 (32-ounce) bottle vegetable juice
1 (14½-ounce) can no-salt-added diced tomatoes, undrained
¼ cup red wine vinegar
1 teaspoon hot sauce
⅛ teaspoon pepper

1 Combine all ingredients, stirring well. Position knife blade in food processor bowl; add one-third of vegetable mixture. Process 30 seconds or until smooth. Transfer mixture to a bowl. Repeat procedure twice with remaining mixture. Cover and chill at least 3 hours. **Yield: 9 (1-cup) servings.**

Per Serving: Calories 42 (6% from fat)   Fat 0.3g (Sat 0.1g)   Protein 1.5g   Carbohydrate 9.8g   Fiber 0.9g   Cholesterol 0mg   Sodium 380mg

■ This tomato soup needs to chill at least three hours to let the flavors combine, but it tastes even better if it chills overnight.

French Onion Soup

Prep: 10 minutes   Cook: 30 minutes

Butter-flavored vegetable cooking spray
1 tablespoon reduced-calorie margarine
3 medium-size sweet onions, thinly sliced
3 cups canned no-salt-added beef broth
1 tablespoon low-sodium Worcestershire sauce
¼ teaspoon salt
¼ teaspoon pepper
2 tablespoons dry sherry
4 (¾-inch-thick) slices French bread, toasted
¼ cup (1 ounce) shredded Gruyère cheese

1 Coat a Dutch oven with cooking spray; add margarine. Place over medium-high heat until margarine melts. Add onion; sauté 5 minutes or until tender. Add broth and next 3 ingredients. Bring to a boil; cover, reduce heat, and simmer 20 minutes. Stir in sherry.

2 Ladle soup into individual 2-cup ovenproof bowls; place bowls on a baking sheet. Top each serving with a slice of bread. Sprinkle cheese evenly over bread. Bake at 300° for 10 minutes or until cheese melts. **Yield: 4 (1¼-cup) servings.**

Per Serving: Calories 221 (22% from fat)   Fat 5.5g (Sat 1.8g)   Protein 7.3g   Carbohydrate 34.4g   Fiber 3.6g   Cholesterol 9mg   Sodium 403mg

■ Gruyère cheese is similar to Swiss cheese, but it has a little sharper flavor. Swiss is a good substitute.

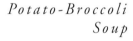 For a touch of "heat," stir ¼ teaspoon dried crushed red pepper into the soup just before serving.

Potato-Broccoli Soup

Prep: 12 minutes   Cook: 25 minutes

3 cups peeled, cubed potato (about 1 pound)
1 cup frozen chopped broccoli, thawed
½ cup chopped carrot
½ cup water
¼ teaspoon salt
1 (14¼-ounce) can no-salt-added chicken broth
1½ cups 1% low-fat milk
3 tablespoons all-purpose flour
6 ounces reduced-fat loaf process cheese spread, cubed
Dried crushed red pepper (optional)
Dried red chile peppers (optional)

1 Combine first 6 ingredients in a large Dutch oven. Bring to a boil; cover, reduce heat, and simmer 20 minutes.

2 Combine milk and flour, stirring until smooth. Add milk mixture and cheese to vegetable mixture in Dutch oven. Cook over medium heat, stirring constantly, until cheese melts and mixture thickens. If desired, sprinkle with crushed pepper and garnish with a dried red pepper.
Yield: 7 (1-cup) servings.

Per Serving: Calories 153 (19% from fat)   Fat 3.3g (Sat 2.1g)   Protein 9.4g Carbohydrate 22.0g   Fiber 2.0g   Cholesterol 11mg   Sodium 484mg

Potato-Broccoli Soup

Spicy Tomato-Corn Chowder

Prep: 5 minutes   Cook: 25 minutes

Vegetable cooking spray
2 teaspoons roasted garlic-flavored vegetable oil
1 (10-ounce) package frozen whole-kernel corn, thawed
1½ teaspoons dried basil
1 (14¼-ounce) can no-salt-added chicken broth
1 (10¾-ounce) can reduced-fat, reduced-sodium tomato soup
½ teaspoon hot sauce
¼ teaspoon salt
¼ teaspoon pepper
Nonfat sour cream (optional)

1 Coat a large saucepan with cooking spray; add oil, and place over medium-high heat until hot. Add corn and basil; sauté 2 minutes. Add broth and next 4 ingredients. Bring to a boil; cover, reduce heat, and simmer 20 minutes. Top each serving with sour cream, if desired.
Yield: 4 (1-cup) servings.   *(Chowder pictured on page 12.)*

Per Serving: Calories 140 (26% from fat)   Fat 4.0g (Sat 0.7g)   Protein 3.4g
Carbohydrate 24.8g   Fiber 2.4g   Cholesterol 0mg   Sodium 385mg

■ The roasted garlic-flavored oil adds a robust flavor to the chowder, but 2 teaspoons of regular vegetable oil may be substituted for the flavored oil.

Minestrone

Prep: 10 minutes   Cook: 50 minutes

Vegetable cooking spray
1 (10-ounce) package frozen chopped onion, celery, and pepper
      blend, thawed
4 (14¼-ounce) cans no-salt-added beef broth
1 (16-ounce) package frozen vegetables with zucchini, cauliflower,
      carrots, and beans, thawed
1 (14½-ounce) can Italian-style tomatoes, undrained and chopped
½ teaspoon dried basil
¼ teaspoon salt
¼ teaspoon pepper
1 cup small pasta shells, uncooked
¼ cup plus 3 tablespoons freshly grated Parmesan cheese

1 Coat a Dutch oven with cooking spray; place over medium-high heat until hot. Add 10-ounce package vegetable blend; sauté 5 minutes. Add broth and next 5 ingredients. Bring to a boil; cover, reduce heat, and simmer 30 minutes. Add pasta; simmer 15 minutes or until pasta is tender. Sprinkle each serving with 1 tablespoon cheese.
Yield: 7 (1½-cup) servings.

Per Serving: Calories 136 (10% from fat)   Fat 1.5g (Sat 0.8g)   Protein 6.7g
Carbohydrate 21.5g   Fiber 3.0g   Cholesterol 3mg   Sodium 477mg

■ *Minestrone* is Italian for "big soup" and usually refers to a thick vegetable soup with pasta and beans. This big soup is quick and easy to prepare because you use canned tomatoes and frozen vegetables.

This chunky vegetable combo is a souped-up version of ratatouille—an eggplant and tomato side dish. Using some canned vegetables along with the fresh makes this soup quick and convenient.

Ratatouille Soup

Prep: 15 minutes Cook: 30 minutes

2½ cups peeled, cubed eggplant (about 1 medium)
2 cups water
2 (14½-ounce) cans no-salt-added whole tomatoes, undrained and
    chopped
1 (4-ounce) can sliced mushrooms, drained
2 cloves garlic, minced
1 medium zucchini, coarsely chopped
1 teaspoon dried Italian seasoning
½ teaspoon salt
¼ teaspoon pepper
½ cup freshly grated Parmesan cheese

1 Combine first 9 ingredients in a Dutch oven, stirring well. Bring to a boil; cover, reduce heat, and simmer 25 minutes or until vegetables are tender. To serve, ladle soup into individual bowls; sprinkle evenly with cheese.
Yield: 8 (1-cup) servings.

Per Serving: Calories 63 (29% from fat) Fat 2.0g (Sat 1.2g) Protein 4.3g
Carbohydrate 8.4g Fiber 1.4g Cholesterol 5mg Sodium 300mg

Ratatouille Soup

Santa Fe Bean Soup

Prep: 5 minutes   Cook: 35 minutes

3   (14¼-ounce) cans no-salt-added beef broth
1   (16-ounce) can no-salt-added pinto beans, drained
1   (15-ounce) can no-salt-added red kidney beans, drained
1   (10-ounce) can chopped tomatoes and green chiles,
       undrained
1   (6-ounce) can no-salt-added tomato paste
1   teaspoon liquid smoke
1   cup (4 ounces) shredded reduced-fat sharp Cheddar cheese

1 Combine first 6 ingredients in a large Dutch oven. Bring to a
boil; reduce heat, and simmer, uncovered, 30 minutes. To serve, ladle
soup into individual bowls; sprinkle evenly with cheese.
Yield: 7 (1-cup) servings.

Per Serving: Calories 235 (14% from fat)   Fat 3.7g (Sat 1.9g)   Protein 15.6g
Carbohydrate 33.3g   Fiber 5.2g   Cholesterol 11mg   Sodium 305mg

■ Dinner's just a can opener away with this easy bean soup.

Black Bean Soup

Prep: 15 minutes   Cook: 50 minutes

3   (15-ounce) cans no-salt-added black beans, drained
2   (14¼-ounce) cans no-salt-added chicken broth
1   cup chopped onion
1   cup chopped sweet red pepper
2   cloves garlic, minced
½   pound extra-lean cooked ham, diced
¾   teaspoon dried oregano
½   teaspoon pepper
¼   teaspoon salt

1 Combine first 5 ingredients in a Dutch oven; bring to a boil.
Cover, reduce heat, and simmer 30 minutes.

2 Transfer 2 cups bean mixture to container of an electric blender
or food processor; cover and process until smooth. Return pureed
bean mixture to Dutch oven. Add ham and remaining ingredients.
Bring to a boil; reduce heat, and simmer, uncovered, 20 minutes or
until thickened.
Yield: 8 (1-cup) servings.

Per Serving: Calories 164 (12% from fat)   Fat 2.1g (Sat 0.6g)   Protein 13.4g
Carbohydrate 22.2g   Fiber 3.9g   Cholesterol 15mg   Sodium 418mg

■ Pureeing some of the bean mixture is a quick, flavorful, and low-fat way to thicken a bean soup.

During the holidays, use your leftover turkey instead of chicken in this soup.

Spinach-Chicken Noodle Soup

Prep: 5 minutes   Cook: 35 minutes

4 (14¼-ounce) cans no-salt-added chicken broth
1 cup chopped onion
1 cup sliced carrot
2 (10½-ounce) cans reduced-fat, reduced-sodium cream of chicken soup
1 (10-ounce) package frozen chopped spinach, thawed
4 cups chopped cooked chicken (skinned before cooking and cooked without salt)
2 cups medium egg noodles, uncooked
½ teaspoon salt
½ teaspoon pepper

1 Combine first 3 ingredients in a Dutch oven. Bring to a boil; cover, reduce heat, and simmer 15 minutes. Add cream of chicken soup and remaining ingredients. Bring to a boil; reduce heat, and simmer, uncovered, 15 minutes.
Yield: 8 (1½-cup) servings.

Per Serving: Calories 227 (23% from fat)   Fat 5.9g (Sat 1.7g)   Protein 22.0g   Carbohydrate 18.9g   Fiber 2.3g   Cholesterol 71mg   Sodium 388mg

Spinach-Chicken Noodle Soup

■ Use leftover chicken or roasted chicken from the grocery store deli in this hearty gumbo.

Easy Chicken Gumbo

Prep: 15 minutes   Cook: 45 minutes

¾ cup all-purpose flour
Vegetable cooking spray
1 (10-ounce) package frozen chopped onion, celery, and pepper blend
5 (14¼-ounce) cans no-salt-added chicken broth
2 teaspoons salt-free Creole seasoning
1 teaspoon pepper
½ teaspoon salt
3½ cups chopped cooked chicken (skinned before cooking and cooked without salt)
1 (10-ounce) package frozen sliced okra, thawed
4 cups cooked long-grain rice (cooked without salt or fat)

1 Place flour in a 15- x 10- x 1-inch jellyroll pan. Bake at 400° for 10 to 15 minutes or until flour is caramel colored, stirring every 5 minutes. Set aside.

2 Coat a large Dutch oven with cooking spray; place over medium-high heat until hot. Add vegetable blend; sauté until tender. Sprinkle with browned flour; stir in broth. Add Creole seasoning, pepper, and salt. Bring to a boil; reduce heat, and simmer, uncovered, 20 minutes. Add chicken and okra; cook 20 minutes. Serve over rice.
Yield: 8 (1½-cup) servings.

Per Serving: Calories 300 (14% from fat)   Fat 4.5g (Sat 1.2g)   Protein 21.0g
Carbohydrate 39.2g   Fiber 1.1g   Cholesterol 50mg   Sodium 211mg

Flour Power

Thicken gumbo the low-fat way with browned flour.

Sprinkle the flour evenly in a baking pan or jellyroll pan.

Bake the flour at 400° for 10 to 15 minutes or until it's a light brown-caramel color.

Seafood Gumbo

Prep: 20 minutes   Cook: 45 minutes

¼ cup plus 2 tablespoons all-purpose flour
2½ pounds unpeeled medium-size fresh shrimp
4 (14½-ounce) cans no-salt-added stewed tomatoes, undrained
3 cups water
1 tablespoon salt-free Creole seasoning
½ teaspoon salt
¼ teaspoon pepper
1 (16-ounce) package frozen vegetable gumbo mixture
1 (15½-ounce) container fresh Standard oysters, drained
Filé powder (optional)

1 Place flour in a 15- x 10- x 1-inch jellyroll pan. Bake at 400° for 10 to 15 minutes or until flour is caramel colored, stirring every 5 minutes. Set aside.

2 Peel and devein shrimp. Set aside.

3 Combine browned flour, tomato, and next 4 ingredients in a large Dutch oven, stirring well. Bring to a boil; cover, reduce heat, and simmer 15 minutes. Add vegetable gumbo mixture; cover and cook 20 minutes. Add shrimp and oysters; cook 5 minutes or until shrimp turn pink and oyster edges curl. Remove from heat, and sprinkle with filé powder, if desired.
Yield: 8 (2-cup) servings.

Per Serving: Calories 257 (11% from fat)   Fat 3.1g (Sat 0.7g)   Protein 28.8g   Carbohydrate 28.2g   Fiber 2.0g   Cholesterol 188mg   Sodium 418mg

Filé powder is made from dried sassafras leaves and is used to thicken gumbo. Stir the powder into the gumbo after you've removed the gumbo from the heat because cooking filé makes it tough and stringy. The okra in gumbo also thickens it, so your gumbo will still be fairly thick, even without the filé.

This chili is great topped with nonfat sour cream and additional chili powder. One tablespoon of sour cream adds about 10 calories.

White Bean Chili

Prep: 10 minutes   Cook: 25 minutes

Vegetable cooking spray
1 cup chopped onion
1 clove garlic, minced
2 (15-ounce) cans cannellini beans, drained
1 (4-ounce) can chopped green chiles, undrained
2¼ cups canned no-salt-added chicken broth
1½ cups chopped cooked chicken (skinned before cooking and
      cooked without salt)
1 teaspoon chili powder
⅛ teaspoon salt
Nonfat sour cream (optional)
Additional chili powder (optional)

1 Coat a large saucepan with cooking spray; place over medium-high heat until hot. Add onion and garlic; sauté until tender. Add 1 can beans and next 5 ingredients. Mash remaining can beans with a fork; add to chicken mixture in saucepan. Bring to a boil; cover, reduce heat, and simmer 20 minutes. If desired, top with sour cream and chili powder. **Yield: 4 (1½-cup) servings.**

Per Serving: Calories 207 (19% from fat)   Fat 4.3g (Sat 1.0g)   Protein 19.4g
Carbohydrate 19.6g   Fiber 3.3g   Cholesterol 43mg   Sodium 554mg

Look for turkey breakfast sausage in the refrigerator section with the other tubes of breakfast sausage or in the freezer section of the grocery store.

Hearty Sausage-Bean Chili

Prep: 15 minutes   Cook: 25 minutes

1 pound freshly ground raw turkey breakfast sausage
¾ pound lean ground round
1½ cups frozen chopped onion, celery, and pepper blend
2 (15-ounce) cans no-salt-added dark red kidney beans, undrained
2 (14½-ounce) cans no-salt-added stewed tomatoes, undrained
1 (15-ounce) can no-salt-added pinto beans, undrained
1 (15-ounce) can chunky chili tomato sauce

1 Combine first 3 ingredients in a large Dutch oven. Cook over medium-high heat until meat is browned, stirring until it crumbles.

2 Return sausage mixture to Dutch oven; add kidney beans and remaining ingredients. Bring to a boil; reduce heat, and simmer, uncovered, 20 minutes or until thickened, stirring occasionally. **Yield: 7 (1½-cup) servings.**

Per Serving: Calories 298 (26% from fat)   Fat 8.5g (Sat 1.9g)   Protein 26.1g
Carbohydrate 28.6g   Fiber 6.5g   Cholesterol 61mg   Sodium 740mg

About the Recipes

Fat

The recommendation to keep your fat intake at 30 percent of total calories means *30 percent of your total calories for the day.* This doesn't mean that every single food you eat has to be under 30 percent.

Recipes that are over 30 percent calories from fat can still be healthy. For example, salmon is higher in fat than some other types of fish, but the type of fat is omega-3 fat, a healthier kind of fat. And for very low-calorie foods like vegetables, the total amount of fat can be low and still make up a large percentage of the calories.

Here's how the 30 percent recommendation translates to actual fat grams per day:

If you should eat 2000 calories per day . . . you can have up to 67 grams of fat

2000 calories x 30% = 600 calories
600 calories ÷ 9 calories per gram = 67 grams fat

Sodium

When you enjoy the ease of using convenience products, be aware that many of them may be high in sodium, even when they are low in fat and calories. Higher sodium levels are often the trade-off for the speed and ease of using convenience products. If you're watching your sodium intake carefully, read food labels and note the sodium value in the nutrient analysis following each recipe.

The current dietary recommendations advise us to limit our sodium to 2,400 milligrams a day. If you eat a sandwich with 800 milligrams of sodium for lunch, that's about one-third of your recommended sodium intake for the day. Keep that in mind as you make choices for the rest of the day, and try to eat low-sodium foods like fresh fruits and vegetables along with your sandwich.

Daily Nutrition Guide

Use the values from the U.S. Dietary Guidelines in the chart below to determine your daily nutrient needs.

	women ages 25 to 50	women over 50	men over 24
Calories*	2,000	2,000 or less	2,700
Protein	50g	50g or less	63g
Fat	67g or less	67g or less	90g or less
Saturated Fat	22g or less	22g or less	30g or less
Carbohydrate	299g	299g	405g
Fiber	25g to 35g	25g to 35g	25g to 35g
Cholesterol	300mg or less	300mg or less	300mg or less
Sodium	2,400mg or less	2,400mg or less	2,400mg or less

*Calorie requirements vary according to your size, weight, and level of activity. The calorie level in the chart is a general guide; you may need more calories if you are pregnant, breastfeeding, or trying to gain weight, and less if you are trying to lose or maintain weight.

Nutrient Analysis

Use the nutrient analysis following each recipe to see how the recipe fits into your healthy eating plan.

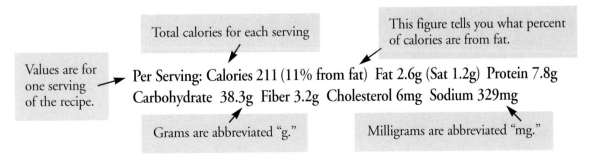

Total calories for each serving

This figure tells you what percent of calories are from fat.

Values are for one serving of the recipe.

Per Serving: Calories 211 (11% from fat) Fat 2.6g (Sat 1.2g) Protein 7.8g
Carbohydrate 38.3g Fiber 3.2g Cholesterol 6mg Sodium 329mg

Grams are abbreviated "g."

Milligrams are abbreviated "mg."

Metric Equivalents

The recipes that appear in this cookbook use the standard United States method for measuring liquid and dry or solid ingredients (teaspoons, tablespoons, and cups). The information in the following charts is provided to help cooks outside the U.S. successfully use these recipes. All equivalents are approximate.

Equivalents for Different Types of Ingredients

A standard cup measure of a dry or solid ingredient will vary in weight depending on the type of ingredient.

A standard cup of liquid is the same volume for any type of liquid. Use the following chart when converting standard cup measures to grams (weight) or milliliters (volume).

Standard Cup	Fine Powder (ex. flour)	Grain (ex. rice)	Granular (ex. sugar)	Liquid Solids (ex. butter)	Liquid (ex. milk)
1	140 g	150 g	190 g	200 g	240 ml
¾	105 g	113 g	143 g	150 g	180 ml
⅔	93 g	100 g	125 g	133 g	160 ml
½	70 g	75 g	95 g	100 g	120 ml
⅓	47 g	50 g	63 g	67 g	80 ml
¼	35 g	38 g	48 g	50 g	60 ml
⅛	18 g	19 g	24 g	25 g	30 ml

Liquid Ingredients by Volume

¼ tsp							1 ml	
½ tsp							2 ml	
1 tsp							5 ml	
3 tsp	=	1 tbls			=	½ fl oz	=	15 ml
		2 tbls	=	⅛ cup	=	1 fl oz	=	30 ml
		4 tbls	=	¼ cup	=	2 fl oz	=	60 ml
		5⅓ tbls	=	⅓ cup	=	3 fl oz	=	80 ml
		8 tbls	=	½ cup	=	4 fl oz	=	120 ml
		10⅔ tbls	=	⅔ cup	=	5 fl oz	=	160 ml
		12 tbls	=	¾ cup	=	6 fl oz	=	180 ml
		16 tbls	=	1 cup	=	8 fl oz	=	240 ml
		1 pt	=	2 cups	=	16 fl oz	=	480 ml
		1 qt	=	4 cups	=	32 fl oz	=	960 ml
						33 fl oz	=	1000 ml = 1 l

Dry Ingredients by Weight

(To convert ounces to grams, multiply the number of ounces by 30.)

1 oz	=	1/16 lb	=	30 g
4 oz	=	¼ lb	=	120 g
8 oz	=	½ lb	=	240 g
12 oz	=	¾ lb	=	360 g
16 oz	=	1 lb	=	480 g

Length

(To convert inches to centimeters, multiply the number of inches by 2.5.)

1 in			=	2.5 cm		
6 in	=	½ ft	=	15 cm		
12 in	=	1 ft	=	30 cm		
36 in	=	3 ft	= 1 yd	=	90 cm		
40 in			=	100 cm	=	1 m

Cooking/Oven Temperatures

	Fahrenheit	Celsius	Gas Mark
Freeze Water	32° F	0° C	
Room Temperature	68° F	20° C	
Boil Water	212° F	100° C	
Bake	325° F	160° C	3
	350° F	180° C	4
	375° F	190° C	5
	400° F	200° C	6
	425° F	220° C	7
	450° F	230° C	8
Broil			Grill

Recipe Index

Acknowledgments

■ ■ ■

Credits

Annieglass, Watsonville, CA
Cassis & Co., New York, NY
Cyclamen Studio, Inc., Berkeley, CA
Droll Designs, Salem, MA
Eigen Arts, Inc., Jersey City, NJ
Fioriware, Zanesville, OH
Karen Alweil Studio, Los Angeles, CA
Lamb's Ears Ltd., Birmingham, AL
Luna Garcia, Venice, CA
Mariposa, Manchester, MA
Peggy Karr Glass, Cedar Knolls, NJ
Southern Settings, Birmingham, AL
Stonefish Pottery, Hartford, CT
Vietri, Hillsborough, NC

■ ■ ■

Source of Nutrient Analysis Data:
Computrition, Inc., Chatsworth, CA and
Information provided by food manufacturers